Lovedon Fields

5 Destination Landscape

6 Learning Outside the Classroom

7 Community

8 The Practice

Glassfields

Introduction by Isabel Allen *(Editor, Architecture Today)*

There was a time when we could see a manicured lawn as a symbol of wholesome domesticity. When we could gaze at a green field and see a rural idyll; a natural counterpart to the artifice of smog-choked city life. When the saturated colours of an unexpected heatwave evoked childhood summers and sun-kissed limbs.

We are learning to adjust our gaze. To see the freshly mown lawn as an assault on biodiversity. To see the green field as a monocultural wasteland; abandoned by wildlife, poisoned by toxins, a victim of commercial agriculture and its relentless appetites. To see intense sunlight as a weapon, set to warm our oceans, threaten our harvests, scorch our skin. We are learning to view the landscape through the prism of environmental degradation. But every loss of innocence goes hand in hand with newfound wisdom. We are learning to understand our landscapes as a physical manifestation of our complex co-existence with the natural world. To view them, not just as picturesque, but as precious, precarious, powerful forces that can have the power to enrich or impoverish the fabric of our lives. The essays in this publication speak eloquently of the benefits of a well crafted landscape: richer habitats for wildlife; higher property values; healthier lifestyles; cleaner air; protection from the ravages of excessive heat or flood.

But the photographs tell another story too; how landscape architecture, at its best, gives us 'new eyes'. A thoughtful composition of plants and trees offers not just light and shade, but infinite permutations of dancing shadows and dappled sunshine; a means of viewing the hard edges of urban life through an altogether softer lens – framed by greenery; filtered by a gauze of rustling leaves and rippled light. A carefully considered landscape prompts us to see a new neighbourhood, not as an alien slice of real estate, but as an integral part of an established landscape. A nuanced public space invites us to understand a patch of common ground as an ecological paradise; a retreat; a space to calibrate interactions with strangers or with friends. To observe – or to participate in, the rituals of civic life. Landscape stitched through the fabric of our day-to-day routine compels us to acknowledge the rhythm of the seasons; the passing of the years; the inevitable cycle of birth, growth and decay.

This book documents a body of work that adds value to development projects, that lifts the spirits, that acts – as the title suggests – as a catalyst for change. But it also paints a portrait of an art form that accentuates the symbiotic relationship between humanity and the natural world; that encourages us to see the world anew.

Isabel Allen is the Editor of Architecture Today and the Editorial Director of BEAM (Built Environment and Architecture Media), founded in 2021 to provide the construction industry with a multi-media platform for interdisciplinary learning and collaboration. Highly experienced in her field, Isabel was previously editor of the AJ and has spearheaded the launch of numerous initiatives including the Architecture Today Awards for buildings that stand the test of time and the Regenerative Architecture Index launched in partnership with Architects Declare.

Alongside a career as an editor, curator and critic she also co-founded HAB Housing, which delivered low-cost housing using natural materials and innovative models of procurement, land ownership and finance. She is an Honorary Fellow of the RIBA.

Isabel Allen *(Editor, Architecture Today)*

"The real voyage of discovery consists not in seeking new landscapes but in having new eyes."

Marcel Proust

1 Public Realm

Cardinal Place

Cardinal Place shopping centre can be found in the heart of Victoria, London - originally completed in 2006. The development marked Landsec's first steps in transforming this city hub into a vibrant place to live, work, shop and socialise. Home to department stores, restaurants, shops and a rooftop public garden, Landsec appointed BD to revitalise Cardinal's public realm in 2022.

For our Stage 1 briefing work on Cardinal, we proposed a strategy of incremental changes to the Estate, allowing interventions in the urban realm to be reviewed and assessed at each level. This allowed the project a level of design fluidity so that aspirations could be adjusted and evolved later down the line – for example in response to community, tenant or artist feedback.

As part of this initial work, we developed a series of instant-impact 'test bed' options for Landsec to trial. These included pop-up Vestre furniture under permitted development rights to test a gateway layout, alongside colourful vinyl floor markings. This was followed by the repainting and replanting of existing site planters in a new colour and planting palette. The results were brilliant: local office workers suddenly lounged in newly found sunny spots; young people had somewhere to chat and socialise; local shoppers and children took a breather amongst the new planting. The newly painted planters happened in 2023 and were a catalyst for starting conversations during the public engagement sessions. The feedback from these test beds was invaluable as we came to develop the detailed permanent design.

> "We have loved working on Cardinal Place – a testament to what thoughtful, engagement-led urban realm renewal can achieve."
>
> Rob Beswick (Founder & Director, BD)

Our concept for the urban realm follows 4 key aims:

1. Capture people's attention: we wanted to play with the gateways of the space and signpost visitors inside. Cardinal is more than just a shopping centre - it is a place with a public offering.

2. Draw them in: once enticed in, we wanted to invite people to explore further.

3. Encourage people to stay: we wanted to create interactive, multipurpose spaces, where one can either observe or directly participate in performance, play, and fun.

4. And encourage them to return: offer flexible spaces that will accommodate a lively, changing programme of activities, social events and happenings.

Cardinal Place

AGO
BUCKINGHAM
Zizzi
MOZZARELLA GARLIC BREAD
PASTA CRISPS

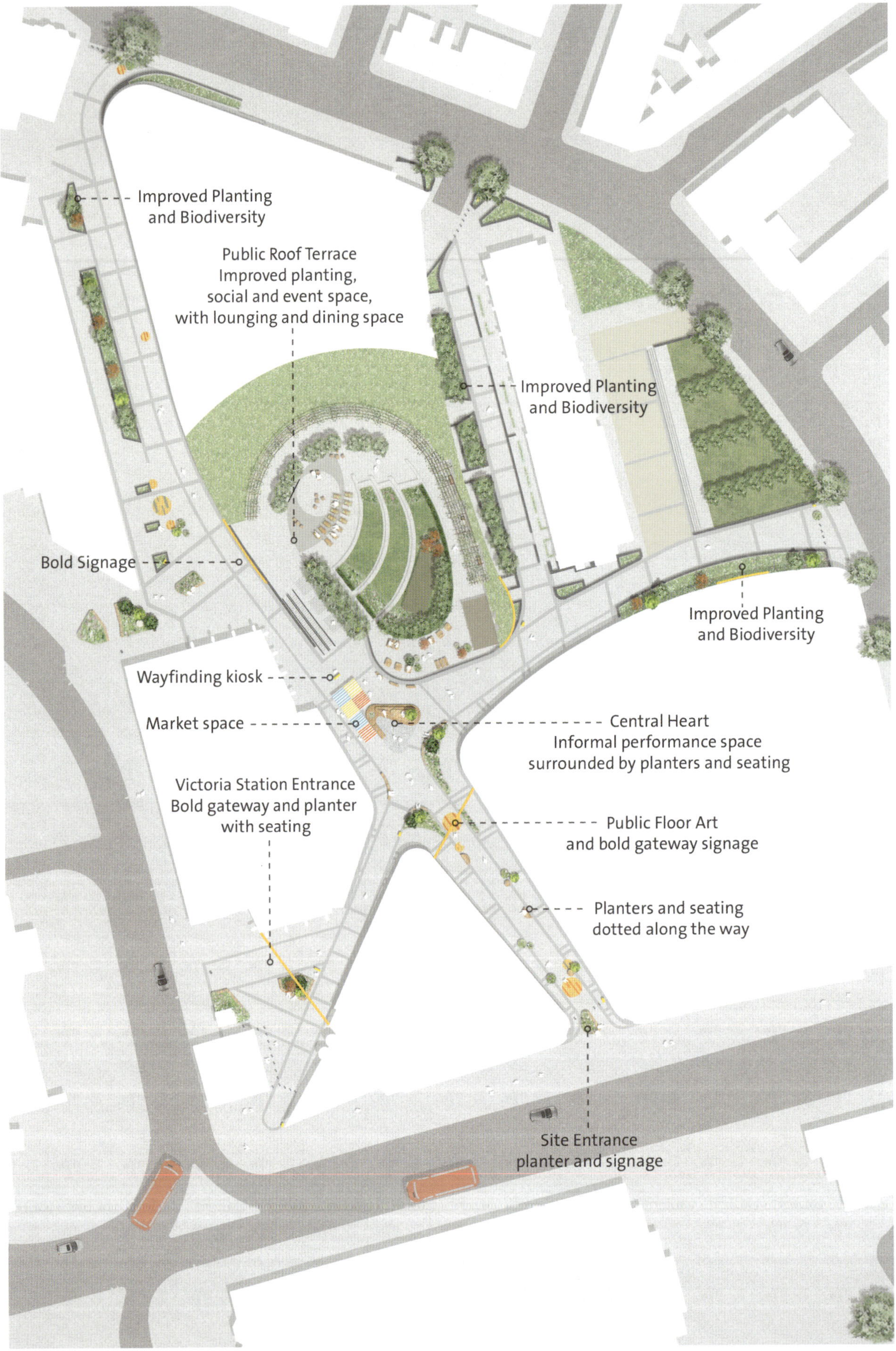
Improved Planting
and Biodiversity
Public Roof Terrace
Improved planting,
social and event space,
with lounging and dining space
Improved Planting
and Biodiversity
Bold Signage
Improved Planting
and Biodiversity
Wayfinding kiosk
Market space
Central Heart
Informal performance space
surrounded by planters and seating
Victoria Station Entrance
Bold gateway and planter
with seating
Public Floor Art
and bold gateway signage
Planters and seating
dotted along the way
Site Entrance
planter and signage

As the design developed, we knew that a wide-ranging public engagement process would be essential to create a truly new urban realm, used long into the future – and you can read about this in detail in chapter 7 of this book. As well as public engagement, the developing designs sought feedback from Westminster City Council, retail tenants, the local Designing Out Crime Officer, and an external Security Advisor.

The final design reflects this extensive engagement process, and by utilising the opportunity of Cardinal's wide walkways and views out, provides a captivating, welcoming, and accommodating public realm for all.

The Victoria Street entrance – one of the busiest gateways in but previously set-back and unclear – has been refreshed with brightly-coloured raised planters richly filled with perennials and bulbs. Integrated seating take in the impressive vista towards Westminster Cathedral, and directional signage steers people towards Cardinal's central heart. The Victoria Underground and Cathedral Walk entrances also feature new raised planters, climbing plants to Cardinal's column features, and gateway signage and seating – all carefully curated around the busiest pedestrian flows onsite.

The new central heart features an organic, amphitheatre-style stepped seating and performance space, again making the most of the Cathedral view. New planters filled with flowering perennials, evergreen shrubs and semi-mature trees wrap around the food and beverage outlets, creating a sense of enclosure and focusing attention on the heart of the scheme.

The rooftop public garden has also been re-pinned to the Cardinal map with new directional signage inviting people in. Movable colourful loungers and seating create a flexible, social oasis amongst enhanced planting that cascades and climbs over planters and shelters.

The Cardinal colour palette unites all of these spaces, and was selected in co-ordination with young people at the engagement sessions. It has lifted the previous monotone to an array of warm and vibrant golds, scarlets and greens which are utilised across signage, wayfinding, planters and furniture. This has created a distinctive and coherent character to Cardinal Place, whilst also aligning sensitively with the wider area's branding.

We have loved working on Cardinal Place – a testament to what thoughtful, engagement-led urban realm renewal can achieve.

Cardinal Place

OMINE·JESU·REX·ET·REDEMPTOR
ER·SANGUINEM·TUUM·SALVA·NOS

It was a pleasure to work with a client who placed such a high value on the landscape and its impact on user experience of the space. The vision of the team at Landsec helped to drive the regeneration forwards and ensured the wider business bought in to our ambitious proposals. The genuine collaboration with the different stakeholders is evident in how the designs developed and it was a joy to undertake, in particular, the input of the young people. The final scheme reflects the aspirations of the client to create a distinctive and memorable landscape that connects to the wider Victoria streetscape.

Emma Santamaria (Senior Associate, BD)

CARDINAL PLACE
TODAY STARTED 11 HOURS AND 29 MINUTES
INFORMATION

The Green Spine

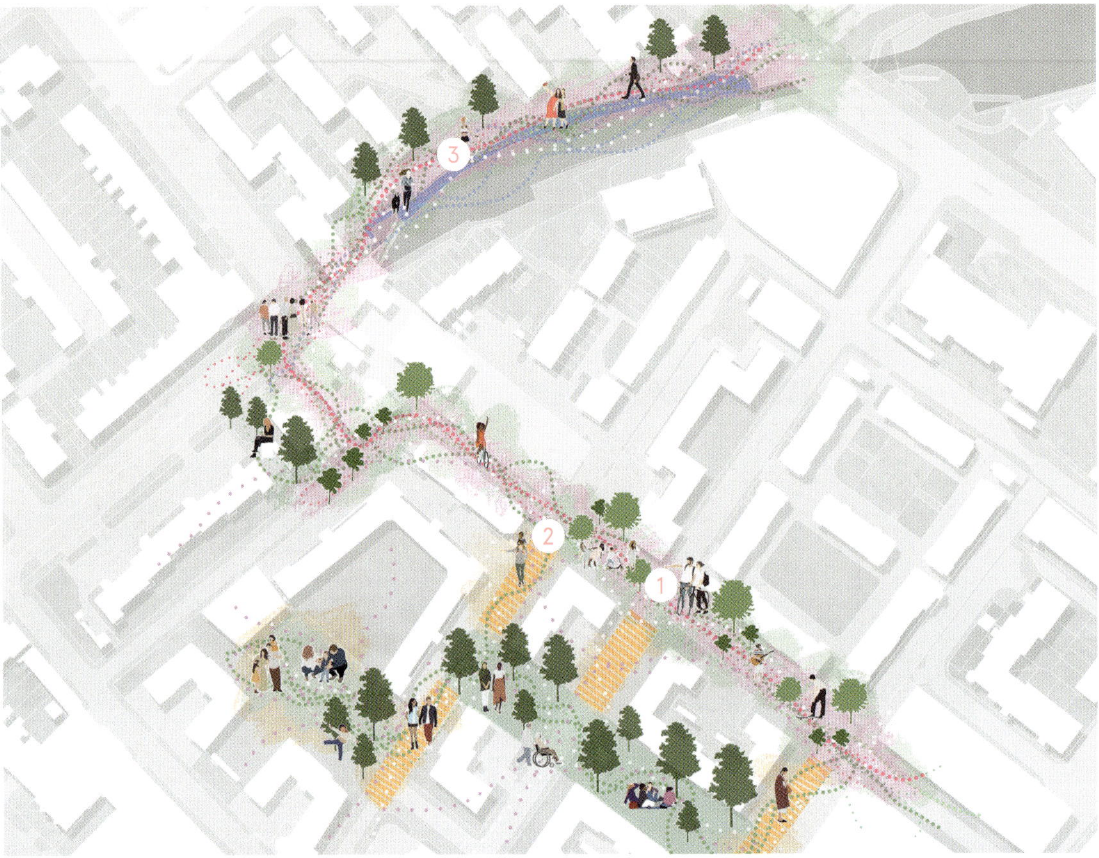

The Green Spine passes through the residential heart of Lisson Grove in the City of Westminster. Building on the success of Phase 1, the extended spine will connect Marylebone Station and Edgware Road Underground to the wider pedestrian routes along the Regent's Canal.

The scheme presents a fantastic opportunity for renewed, high-quality public realm that will tie the neighbouring and diverse communities of Lisson Grove together through green infrastructure. The consultation strategy was a kickstart for this, and BD relished the opportunity to work with local groups, key stakeholders and the wider community to examine the existing issues of the urban townscape, and collaborate on new ideas.

Our concept focused on: introducing varied layers of diverse urban greening; traffic-calming; and joyful playable trails.

We have proposed cherished 'Green Links' as central oases to envelop residents in trees, raingardens and naturalistic planting. 'Living Streets' run off these and propose a shift of focus from cars to people – introducing traffic-calming and rationalised car parking to encourage a walkable community, with all the benefits of active travel, boosted activity, decreased pollution, plus a more inclusive and sociable public realm.

Playable trails weave through each of the spaces, reinforcing a dynamic character and encouraging people to connect with the wider Green Spine.

The use of a virtual reality model was a highlight of our consultation design process, giving opportunity for the public to visualise the before and after of the richly reimagined public realm proposals.

1

2

3

All Saints Street

Regent's Wharf lies tucked between the historic Regent's Canal and All Saints Street in bustling King's Cross London. The project for Bentall Green Oak has revamped a series of canal-side warehouses into modern, high-spec office accommodation, sensitively designed by Hawkins\Brown.

The urban history of the site and its proximity to this serene part of the Regent's Canal provided us with rich concepts for the landscape; we drew inspiration from the varied industrial textures of existing stone setts and cobbles, the existing trees and indigenous planting, and waterside wildlife of moorhens and bats in the local area.

The renovation of the built form has created three distinct courtyards that wrap around the warehouses and meet the Canal to the northern side of site: Thorley Gardens, Shadbolt Square, and Bartlett Yard.

Thorley Gardens has been designed as an urban oasis for tenants at the Wharf, with views across the Regent's Canal. The gardens are lushly planted and peppered with inclusive seating pockets designed for all; creating a quiet, restful space amongst the energy of the city.

Shadbolt Square channels that energy into a generous, bustling public space at the heart of the site which is overlooked by Victorian walkways and newly planted specimen pine tree as a central landmark.

Bartlett Yard runs between The Mill building and its nearest neighbour. Richly planted soft landscape beds direct the eye to a framed vista of Regent's Canal and draw the serenity and sounds of the water through the yard.

The project was opened in 2024 with BD involved from concept design right up to completion.

All Saints Street

"We are delighted with the potential of the realised project to significantly improve the experience and wellbeing of workers and visitors – with a serene biophilic atmosphere, where abundant lush planting and views across the canal bring one closer to nature."

Nikki Petrova (Senior Landscape Architect, BD)

Wandsworth Gasworks

"This site has long sat empty and unused in the centre of one of the most well connected and desirable parts of London. We are proud to have been able to secure a future for the site that will benefit both existing and new residents, and provide space for the hugely important local music industry."

Steve Sanham (Founding Director, Common Projects)

The 3.5 acre Gasworks regeneration site lies across the urban River Wandle, railway viaduct and the dual carriageway of Wandsworth's Swandon Way – a complex industrial hotchpotch that currently turns its back on its meandering neighbour.

BD have been working on this ambitious urban scheme since 2020, alongside an award-winning design team including SHEDkm, Max Architects, Carmody Groarke and engineers Whitby Wood. SGN Place and Mitheridge Capital Management set the brief for a major residential-led mixed-use scheme, including 700 new homes for the London Borough.

The site presents an amazing opportunity to stitch the Wandle back into its urban context: a new bridge link across the River; an active urban riverside park; and the centrepiece of a new Wandle Trail.

We have designed the Trail to form a strategic link alongside the River - opening up views of mature tree lined banks, naturalised with biodiverse waterside planting, and connecting people on foot and cycle into the wider Gasworks development. Connected pocket play parks will also meander alongside the River, and will celebrate the site's rich industrial and natural heritage through playable mounds, tunnels, slides and revealed gas infrastructure such as the Gasholder Ring Beam.

155 semi-mature trees are proposed along the Wandle Trail and the new street network, which also incorporates public art, social seating, and space for pop-up events. These will lead people up from the River and into the heart of the repurposed gasometer and Gasholder Gardens.

Revealing, celebrating and expanding the green lung of the Wandle will bring huge benefits to the population of Wandsworth – providing breathing space, urban cooling, and biodiversity, as well as up-close glimpses of the Wandle's herons and kingfishers enjoying an expanded habitat.

The scheme is progressing through a co-design process prior to planning.

Wandsworth Gasworks

The Strand

"It was brilliant to see the completed public realm offering flexible space for pop-up events and people taking the opportunity to stop, sit and look out over the harbour or have a photograph with the Agatha Christie sculpture."

Helen Kirk (Senior Associate, BD)

The Strand is a prominent stretch of carriageway on the English Riviera in Torquay, overlooking the Old Harbour. Torbay Council envisaged this previously car-dominated stretch as a revitalised public space, and BD have worked closely with highways and the design team to achieve this vision.

The landscape concept focused on a generously expanded pedestrianised area; reimagined in robust materials inspired by the distinctive historic character of the town; and linking people to the natural beauty of the Tor Bay.

A key aspect has been to bring the grade II listed Clock Tower into the pedestrianised area, which provides a focal point and historic connection - previously lost when surrounded by traffic. Carefully located seating and high quality paving knits the space to its harbour outlook and draws on the historic granite materiality of the area. By keeping the design uncluttered, the series of open spaces also allows the Strand to facilitate a variety of seasonal activities, such as markets and small pop-up events.

The landscape is truly multi-functional, with biodiverse planting beds also forming an integral part of the Strand's Sustainable Drainage System, catching and filtering surface water. A dedicated cycle route is also provided to connect Victoria Parade and Torwood Street to Cary Parade.

BD have enjoyed being a key part of the wider regeneration of Torbay, and have been working over several years with our design team colleagues to bring hard-working, high-quality landscape designs to sites ranging from The Strand, to Abbey Sands public realm, to Paignton Station.

Landscape as a Catalyst

by Romy Rawlings, (Director, Deep Green)

In the built environment, landscape is often viewed as a green garnish, yet its true potential extends far beyond its aesthetic value. Our landscapes, often simply defined as the space between buildings, offer immense opportunities for social, environmental, and economic transformation. When we shape these spaces and leverage their potential through a holistic approach, landscapes can act as powerful catalysts for positive change.

The Role of Landscapes in Urban Settings

As global population creeps inexorably towards an estimated 9.8 billion by 2050, and urbanisation increases in parallel, our outdoor spaces will play an increasingly critical role. They must address the most pressing and complex challenges of climate change and biodiversity loss by transforming from car dominated streets and neglected corners into truly sustainable places where people choose to live, work, and visit.

The United Nations' Sustainable Development Goal 11 highlights the need for cities to integrate more public spaces to support citizens' health and wellbeing. The target is for 45-50% of cities to be dedicated to public spaces and streets by 2030, yet on average, cities comprise less than 20% of such spaces. This huge gap highlights not only the need for greater investment in landscapes, but also the enormous opportunities that exist.

Balancing People, Planet, and Profit

At the heart of landscape architecture lies the principle of sustainability. This is often encapsulated by the concept of balancing three key components, or pillars: People, Planet, and Profit (or Purpose). This framework fosters a holistic approach, recognising that focusing solely on one aspect at the expense of the others can have unintended negative consequences.

Landscapes are immensely complex and capable of delivering multiple simultaneous benefits and, when thoughtfully planned, the scope to make a positive impact is vast. Absolutely integral to shaping how places function socially, environmentally, and economically, the public spaces we craft should be viewed as essential infrastructure. Whether parks, green corridors, or city squares, these places are vital components of daily lives.

However, as we see all too frequently, prioritising economic gains over environmental or social factors can result in poorly executed landscapes that fail to deliver long-term benefits. In our essentially capitalist economy, profitability remains a primary motivator and, without a solid business case for investing in landscape, projects are often 'value engineered' to a mere shadow of their original potential. And, even when the original investment is maintained, much is often lost due to a lack of management and ongoing care.

While budgets must of course be balanced, this focus on short-term savings often undermines the long-term potential of a landscape. And, let's face it, very little is more 'long-term' than trees, particularly much needed long lived species such as oak. Poorly designed and executed landscapes, whether due to underfunding or neglect, will likely fail to deliver their intended benefits. Worse still, they may even be viewed as counterproductive if they are seen to encourage antisocial behaviour and other societal ills. The good news is that there is considerable evidence proving that investment in quality landscapes provides significant economic returns. When professionally designed and installed, landscapes improve property values by stimulating demand, support local economies, increase tourism, and mitigate costly risks from flooding or excessive heat. In addition, they support environmental and social benefits that far exceed the financial outlay.

People, Place, and Nature: A Framework for Landscape Benefits

The Landscape Institute's framework of 'People, Place, and Nature' provides a comprehensive approach to understanding the multifaceted benefits of great landscapes. Each element plays a crucial role in creating thriving, resilient, and liveable spaces.

People — Communities are the heart of any landscape. Well-designed public spaces foster social cohesion, and provide opportunities for interaction, recreation, and active living. They also contribute to community engagement since age, gender and background need not be barriers to fostering connections. Landscape interventions can also help address the issue of food security through urban agriculture initiatives, allotments, and community gardens. Moreover, these spaces are vital for public health, contributing to both mental and physical wellbeing.

Place — A successful place is more than simply a functional space: it has its own unique identity. The built and natural environments of a community shape its character and, through the additional layers of history and culture, landscapes are deeply entwined with a sense of place. Thoughtfully designed places encourage emotional connections that enhance the quality of life for residents and visitors alike. They increase both foot traffic and dwell time, delivering economic value by attracting businesses, tourism, and consequently further investment.

Nature — Nature is a vital component of almost every landscape. Integrating natural elements, such as trees, plants, and water mitigates the impact of climate change. Green infrastructure reduces urban heat islands (also lowering energy consumption), improves air quality, manages stormwater and reduces the risk of flooding, and promotes biodiversity. In addition, parks and green space offer recreational opportunities that encourage healthier lifestyles. This is all fundamental in urban environments, where access to nature may be almost non-existent, yet is much needed to support the wellbeing of city dwellers.

Addressing Social Crises: The Transformative Power of Green Spaces

The profound connection between landscape and health is increasingly recognised as one of the most compelling reasons to invest in green spaces. Access to quality landscapes directly benefits our health, whether through improved physical fitness or supporting mental wellbeing.

The positive effects of green spaces on health are so significant that the UK government has recognised the potential cost savings for the National Health Service (NHS). According to the Environment Agency, universal access to green spaces could save the NHS billions of pounds annually in treatment costs. In terms of social benefits, landscapes play a crucial role in enhancing the quality of life for individuals and communities. Studies show that spending time in nature reduces stress, lowers blood pressure, reduces the risk of heart disease, and improves cognitive function. In terms of mental health, studies have shown that access to green spaces can reduce anxiety and depression by up to 30% in urban populations.

In addition, outdoor spaces help reduce social isolation and foster community cohesion, both of which are essential for improved health outcomes. Social isolation is reduced when safe places are provided for people to gather, play, exercise, relax, and interact; this is particularly beneficial for potentially vulnerable groups such as the elderly, women, children, and low-income citizens. This point on equity is key. In many cities, marginalised communities, and particularly those in deprived areas, have limited access to green space. The disparity in proximity to nature is often stark and it's widely accepted that these bleak, nature-deprived environments contribute to higher rates of poor physical and mental health. When we prioritise the provision of green space in underserved areas, this alone can significantly 'level up' society. As urban populations continue to grow, equitable access to nature becomes ever more urgent.

The Evidence: Landscape as a Catalyst for Change

There are many superb examples of projects that demonstrate the catalytic power of the landscape. Internationally, Barcelona's 'Superblocks' are transforming congested streets into car-free zones that are filled with parks, play, and spaces in which to linger. Barcelona has seen a significant increase in social interactions, healthier lifestyles, and environmental benefits such as reduced air pollution and heat island effects. The city's residents are estimated to have an increased life expectancy of over six months due to the health benefits that have been delivered.

Surely everyone is aware of the incredible success of New York's High Line, a once-abandoned elevated railway that has been transformed into a public park. It is a project that is being emulated all over the world, due to its huge success. Since its opening, the High Line has become a symbol of urban regeneration, attracting millions of visitors and stimulating billions of dollars of new development in the surrounding area. The park has become a focal point for both residents and tourists, providing an oasis of greenery in the heart of the city and demonstrating the economic and social value of integrating nature into urban spaces. Closer to home, established London-based projects such as Kings Cross and Elephant Park demonstrate the value of a long-term investment strategy with landscape at its heart. BD Landscape has played a part in both, and their contributions to these exemplar projects can be seen in chapters two and five of this book.

Conclusion: Harnessing the Full Potential of Landscapes

As we face the ever-increasing planetary and societal challenges of today, the role of landscape has never been more critical. Far from being merely decorative, landscapes are powerful tools that can catalyse positive change across multiple dimensions. Whether we're designing vibrant public spaces to foster social cohesion, improving environmental resilience to mitigate climate change, or generating sustainable economic growth, landscapes deliver wide-ranging and innovative solutions.

To realise their full potential, we must ensure that green spaces are accessible and available to all. By doing so, we can craft places that are more liveable, equitable, and resilient. No longer can landscape be viewed as a luxury or an afterthought, but as a crucial component of sustainable development that will transform communities for generations to come.

Romy Rawlings is a freelance consultant, specialising in sustainable landscapes and placemaking, with 30 years' experience in the built environment sector. She has spent half of her career as a practicing landscape architect and the other half working with landscape manufacturers across the UK and Europe.

Romy has a comprehensive understanding of the materials, manufacturing processes, and logistics that shape sustainable landscape materials. She is deeply committed to advocating for equity within the sector and firmly believes that high quality landscape design and delivery can significantly enhance societal well-being. A regular speaker and writer, Romy is passionate about advancing sustainable practices and raising awareness of the importance of responsible design in the built environment.

2 Making the Meanwhile

The King's Cross Pond Club

"if not the hottest, the new pond at King's Cross is without doubt London's coolest new attraction'

Adrian Bridge, The Telegraph

The Pond Club was the definition of a meanwhile landscape: open fleetingly between May 2015 and September 2016, but with a huge impact greater than the sum of its parts. It proudly occupied the heart of Lewis Cubitt Park as King's Cross transformed through the 2010s, dazzling between the development plots and site hoardings.

BD were appointed by Argent to take Ooze Architects' concept for the UK's first natural public swimming pool through the planning process. The scheme was initially envisaged as a living art installation, and devised as part of the RELAY King's Cross public art programme. Following planning success, we took on the design team lead and enjoyed working closely with CCS, Willerby Landscapes, PBA and specialist water designers Kingcombe Aquacare during the Club's construction phases.

The 40m-long pond was designed to accommodate over 100 bathers, and was entirely chemical free. The water was purified through a natural, closed-loop process where marginal, aquatic, and oxygenating plants across about a half of the pool's surface filtered and cleaned the water for swimmers. Both the landscape and the pool installation itself utilised a number of recycled materials from the industrial brownfield site including granite cobbles and kerbs.

Framed by colourful wildflowers and textured grasses, the pond's setting changed with every season of its use, and evolved alongside the luscious aquatic planting. This dreamy setting coaxed in over 20,000 visitors during the pond's lifetime, providing peace and the invigorating benefits of cool water within the urban hubbub of King's Cross.

The Pond Club was dismantled after two years as planned, but not before a campaign of local swimmers and dippers attempted to save it. We too really miss the opportunity for a spot of wild swimming in the capital, and hope that this pioneering scheme has and will continue to inspire meanwhile schemes to think adventurously – and in time, influence some permanent counterparts.

Pond Club

"This groundbreaking project set an innovative precedent for how public swimming pools could be conceived and delivered."

Landscape Institute Judges' comments
Overall Winner for 2017 'Design for a Temporary Landscape'

ZONE 3
ZONE 2
ZONE 1

Glassfields

Between Bristol Temple Meads station and the city's Castle Park, Glassfields is a major redevelopment quarter of four previously brownfield plots. Royal London Asset Management (RLAM) asked BD to investigate the possibilities for the long-term landscape design, as well as transform the central local node into a meanwhile park.

Our brief was to provide an inviting and beautiful sanctuary that people can enjoy for a minimum of three years, all whilst surrounding developments are staged and built out. As a major development, RLAM also asked for a harmonised space that could deliver a sense of the Glassfields place – where people could sit, rest and enjoy in this busy urban setting.

Our role began with a site walkover alongside the client, where we identified the boundaries for the future meanwhile park – centrally located between building plots, and capturing pedestrian routes from nearby Old Market, Temple Way and the Floating Harbour.

The opportunity to bring nature back into this brownfield site was golden, and was paired with our research into the layered industrial heritage of the area. Overlooked by the arched windows of former warehouses; the nearby historic Gardiner Haskins site; and with the area's history of bottle making, we had a rich source of inspiration. Alongside the brief to create a biodiverse, central green outlook, these historic motifs fed into the developing designs for a number of bespoke items including eye-catching wayfinding, seating, and temporary hoarding.

To fulfil our vision for brownfield nature, we have introduced an array of soft landscape typologies to provide continuous habitat and visual interest throughout the year. Central to the design are large, striking swathes of native wildflower meadows. These are interwoven with undulating, flowering shrubs and perennials, alongside wildlife stations and birch, cherry and amelanchier tree planting.

As a result, the completed Glassfields park forms a much-needed green oasis within this lively part of the city. Bristolians, alongside their pollinator neighbours, are able to escape the busy streets and find breathing space amongst meadows and sensory planting.

"From our initial meeting BD `just got it'. Their initial response to the brief showed an understanding of the space, the flexibility required and the budget. They slotted into the existing team effortlessly and have been a pleasure to work with."

Heather Hobbs (Project Manager, Heatherhobbs)

Tall, bespoke wayfinding elements and playful, winding paths lead visitors into a central circle at the heart of the park, the forms of which were inspired by the area's connection to glass making and blowing. This heart is lit-up after dark by bespoke weathering steel channels and a Gobo light projector. Two large, curving benches were designed in collaboration with local metalworker Rank Engineering that partly enclose the circle, creating space for flexible pop-up events and socialising. The benches also feature weathering steel, punched through with motifs that reflect our vision for the heritage and brownfield biodiversity of Glassfields.

We also developed high-quality custom seating alongside Bristol furniture designers King & Webbon. These bring a unique sense of place and comfort to the park, encouraging people to pause on their way through, and spill-out from the neighbouring hotel and office buildings. Our designs for the hoardings – custom printed by Bristol's Artwork Solutions – provide a unique and colourful backdrop to the busy thoroughfare.

The programme for meanwhile schemes is often high-paced, and Glassfields was no exception. Having been appointed in early 2020, we saw the project gain planning permission a year later in March 2021, and it was completed early in 2022 by contractor CW Duke. The high-impact of this important pocket park has been celebrated as a finalist in 'Excellence in Place Regeneration' at the 2022 Landscape Institute Awards, and formed part of the nationwide 'People | Place | Nature' Landscape Institute tour of exemplar public realm precedents.

As a meanwhile space, the design had to find a balance between temporary installations and permanent pieces – with the aim that the latter will ultimately be re-used within the final Glassfields masterplan. Our focus on local manufacturers and the defining history of this pocket of Bristol has instilled the park with a strong sense of place, which we hope will be carried long into the future of this site's exciting evolution.

"This is what I enjoy about being a Landscape Architect, particularly being part of the Glassfields wider team to realise the concept design through the construction detailing to create this meaningful meanwhile landscape for people and nature."

Helen Kirk (Senior Associate, BD)

Glassfields

"The project overcomes the site challenges in a creative way and with panache whilst bringing together people and nature, pushing the benefits of what can we achieved in a meanwhile park. It's a commendable effort given the available budget, provides a functional, thoughtful and beautiful space in an environmentally sensitive way. Glassfields maximises the opportunity for local regeneration through a vibrant meanwhile space."

Landscape Institute Judges' comments
Highly commended for 2022 'Excellence in Place Regeneration'

Sayer Street

Congratulations for delivering a great piece of placemaking. Hard work, a really knotty little project but we are delighted with the outcomes and it is great that this is being recognised in the industry too! Thank you!"

Guy Thomas (Head of Place Assets, Lendlease)

A brand new high street in Elephant & Castle - Sayer Street connects leafy Elephant Park to Walworth in the London Borough of Southwark. Perched against the hoardings for a future development for the duration of the construction period, the challenge was to design half a temporary street – only 4 metres wide and 100 metres long – which would respond to the recently opened food and beverage parade opposite.

BD were involved from the outset of the concept stages in 2018 through to completion in 2020, and loved working in collaboration with Jan Kattein Architects, engineers HRW, and lighting designers Michael Grubb Studio. Our brief was to create a unique sense of place, authentic to the creative local community and with opportunity for activation and discovery throughout the day and into the evening.

The outcome was a contemporary reinterpretation of the high street, where we were able to play with the temporary nature of the space through colourful 'floating' planters and decks, and playful scaffold and lighting. The spaces created between and within the canopies became shelters, social and work spaces, with flexible seating complementing the restaurant parade opposite, inspiring passers-by to linger. Sayer Street's playful and vibrant 'jungle' planting palette – full of tall palms, leafy grasses and winding climbers – created an immersive experience and green oasis against its urban jungle backdrop.

The scheme was dismantled in 2024 upon completion of the neighbouring development, with its light-touch materials earmarked for reuse nearby. Its spectacular design and finish won it a 2021 Landscape Institute award for 'Excellence in Place Regeneration', alongside Architect's Journal, NLA New London awards and a Pineapple award from Festival of Place.

“Incredibly innovative and beautifully executed – landscape and architecture come together a functional, cheerful and important place for the growing community to take ownership and foster pride in the completed scheme. The combination of colour, lighting and planting create a unique series of experiences that facilitate a distinctive overall atmosphere that looks to drive both economic and social change.”

Landscape Institute Judges’ comments
Overall Winner for 2021 ‘Excellence in Place Regeneration’

Sayer Street

Warning

The Meadow

As you made your way up Sayer Street, or walked out of Elephant & Castle underground towards the new Elephant Park development, you would have been immersed in the beauty of The Meadow.

Active until 2025; The Meadow was a playful, meanwhile landscape designed for our client Lendlease. It provided a shared sanctuary for people and pollinators within a dense urban environment that is in the midst of huge change and redevelopment.

Integrated with the playful streetscape of Sayer Street next door, our concept for The Meadow was to capture the imagination of all ages; bringing this important node to life through vibrant biodiversity, sculpture, and natural play.

One of our key aims was to encourage and grow our urban pollinator populations. We interwove crucial habitat and foraging opportunities throughout the design: ribbons of wildflower meadow provided by Wildflower Turf, pollen-rich perennial planting and habitat stations.

Working closely with artist Tom Hare, we placed woven willow sculptures throughout. Visitors had a chance to pause and admire the life-sized woven elephant, as well as stop and rest at the towering tulips. These botanical heads nodded to the site's historical use as a Market Garden, as well as highlighting our ecological ambitions of the site for the present.

Site-felled timber and surplus soil was also creatively re-used for natural play trails and tilted landforms. At night, the space was transformed by glowing light installations, designed in collaboration with Michael Grubb Studio, marking the entrance to the park in pops of pink.

The Meadow shared the 2021 Landscape Institute award for `Excellence in Place Regeneration' alongside its sister project Sayer Street and has drawn in thousands of people and pollinators throughout its life.

"Spending a day in the Meadow during the Open House weekend in September 2020 and speaking with local residents and the wider community gave me a great insight into how valuable the space had become during the turbulent months of lockdown from March 2020. This doorstep playable green lung with highlights of seasonal wildflower meadow and cherished public art brought fresh air, play, contact with nature and an uplifting sense of place to so many people."

Rob Beswick (Founder + Director, BD)

P5
THANK YOU

"Making a space in which people look just as beautiful as the spaces do, places in which the lighting changes the atmosphere of the whole environment in the evening and night – and in turn give something rewarding, exciting to visit, spend time, and live around. We feel this type of lighting gives enthusiasm and a unique identity to the place"

Stuart Alexander (Lighting Design Lead, MGS)

The Meadow

COME TO
EPHANT PARK

Milkshake Tree

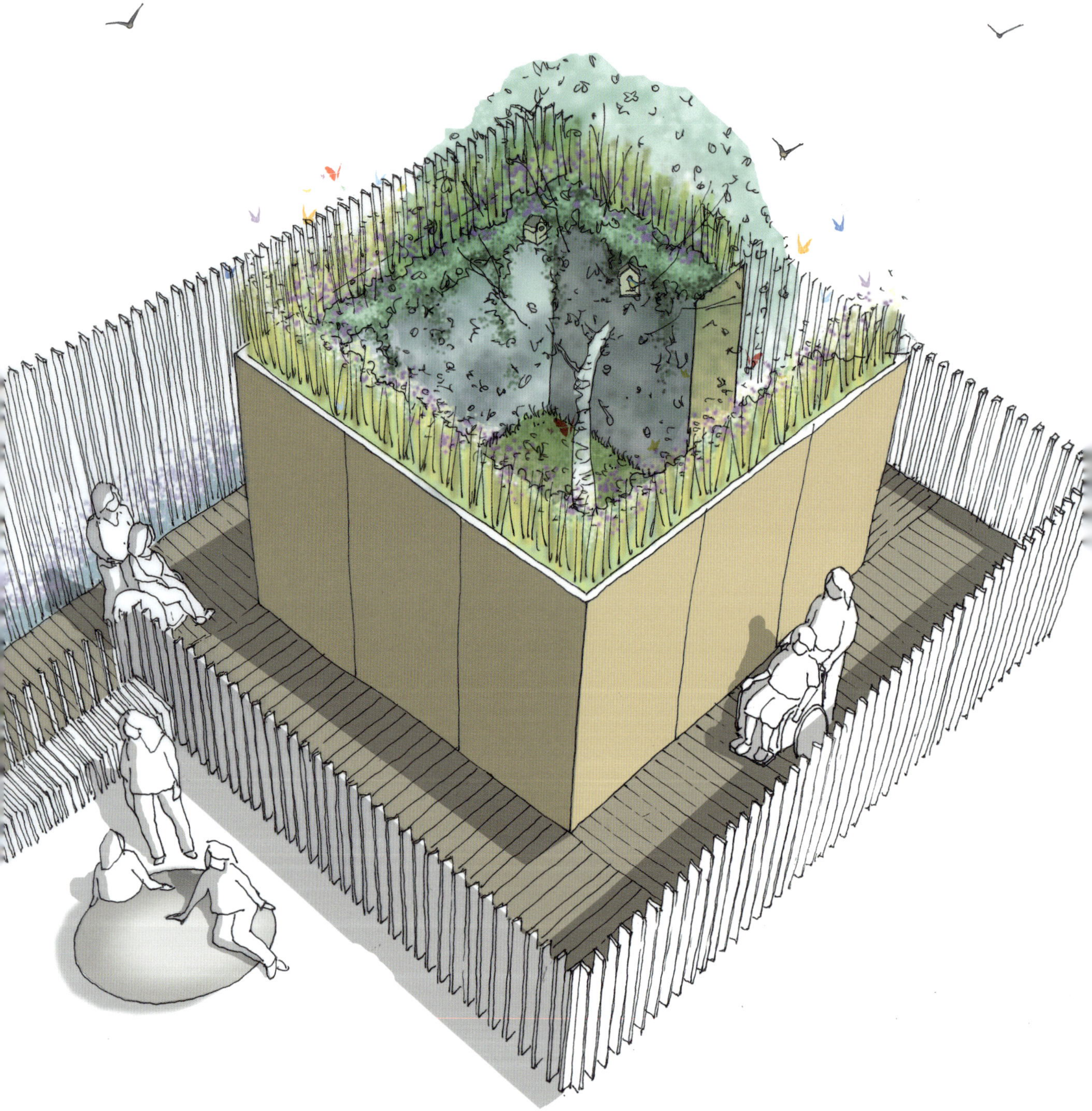

"As a temporary pavilion, it acted as a platform to share and educate the public on environments that help to stimulate, heal and support growth for children with Cerebral Palsy."

Andy Puncher (Lateral Growing Communities)

During our engagement process for the design of a Specialist Cerebral Palsy Centre in Haringey, one child requested a tree that grew milkshakes to be planted in the gardens – and so, The Milkshake Tree was born.

As part of the 2016 London Festival of Architecture, we worked in collaboration with pH+ Architects on this meanwhile installation to promote the important work of the London Centre for Children with Cerebral Palsy (LCCCP). The innovative structure and sensory garden acted as a platform to share, engage and educate the general public on inclusive environments that help to stimulate and support growth.

The Milkshake Tree distilled our design work on LCCCP's planned Specialist Centre: a microcosm of a fully immersive playscape which the public could enjoy. We focused on the use of LCCCP's Conductive Education techniques, turning all parts of a child's day into an immersive learning situation – providing opportunities to practice emerging skills not only during school, but also in the many interconnecting parts of their day.

The installation was built by pH+, BD and collaborators at Peninsula Square, next door to the O2 in Greenwich. Walking up the accessible entrance ramp, children and adults alike were invited to play the musical walkway using a giant xylophone, partly enclosed by a timber screen. Reflective cladding and swaying grasses added to the multisensory experience, with a kids-only den in the heart of the installation centred around an Amelanchier tree.

As well as being a great chance to test the principles of Conductive Learning in landscape, it was fantastic to see hundreds of passers-by play through the installation and celebrate the importance of inclusive design.

Milkshake Tree

The Milkshake Tree

Milkshake Tree

"Growing Communities:" The Importance of Shared Space in the Work of BD Landscape Architects

by Andy Puncher
(Lateral Growing Communities)

"This is my dance space. This is your dance space. I don't go into yours, you don't go into mine. You gotta hold the frame."

Johnny Castle "Dirty Dancing" 1987

Shared Space is the metaphysical, physical and programmatic place where the Self and Other meet and interact. It is the park, square, yard, street, kerb and doorstep of the city as well as the overlaying of use classes to instigate exchange, interaction shared experience and memory. This in turn allows community and, at its largest collective scale, culture and society to form.

In this context it is therefore interesting to analyze Johnny Castle's instructions above which although mechanically important in establishing and maintaining posture, fails to recognize that it is actually the third dance space which their "frame" forms that is the critical one in the success of their Merengee. Psychoanalysis refers to this space as the & in-between" or "creative" space; an intermediate area of shared experience where inner reality and external life interact, creating a space for creativity to develop and Jonny and Baby's legendary, and trophy wining, chemistry to form.

In high quality place making, understanding how to design shared space is paramount in encouraging senses of community ownership and cohesion. This needs to occur at all scales and levels of detail. It requires an understanding that more intimately scaled and heavily programmes spaces, are adopted more immediately as communities begin to form and, with enhanced confidence, the larger more flexible and interpretably programmed, public spaces become inhabited.

As "non sellable" space, the most fundamental shared space of the public realm is often the first area of schemes to be "value engineered" by Developers who, with increasing pressure on public finance, are being entrusted to curate our cities. This is however massively counter intuitive as, it is only through the delivery of high quality and considered "shared spaces", that higher commercial and residential densities can be accommodated and living and working experiences optimised. This optimisation generates higher commercial returns which, in turn, facilitates investment in bespoke contextual responses which can viably accommodate a greater range of often less profitable tenures and uses, creating richer and more robust community structures (and justifiable and so ultimately successful planning strategies).

Shared Space design, and an appreciation of its value, can be seen as central to BD Landscape Architect's work of all scales and it is inspiring and affirming to revisit their built projects to see how they have provided the catalyst for the formation of the communities who have now adopted and tend them.

In their work on Fish Island and Hackney Wick, BD's forensic analysis, interpretation and reworking of the industrial yard brings together, the incumbent Creative and Industrial Communities with the new residential led populations of its regeneration. This seems particularly appropriate in this context as it effectively reestablishes the physical and programmatic blurring of living and working patterns and intensification which are synonymous with its past.

However, it is perhaps through their more temporal projects that the value of shared space and BD's skill in designing and delivering them, can be most graphically observed and documented.

Much has been written about the King's Cross Pond Club which, over only 18 months from its position amidst a city scale building site, provided a public shared space not only for 20,000 open water swimming enthusiasts, but more as a framework for the integration of the incumbent and emerging communities of the locale. For the Developer, further value was delivered as it became an opportunity to present and invite the community. (and future customers) to engage with their ethos and agenda for the development that would ultimately replace it.

On an intensified scale, 'The Milkshake Tree', a volunteer led self-build project realized, with wider community material sponsorship, by BD and the projects Design and Delivery Team, concentrated the potential of shared space even further. As a temporary pavilion, it acted as a platform to share and educate the public on environments that help to stimulate, heal and support growth for children with Cerebral Palsy. However, as a fully accessible public shared space it achieved so much more as a totem for, and opportunity to break down prejudices of, disability bringing together children (and adults) of all abilities through play.

Through this lens, both the King's Cross Pond and Milkshake Tree should not be considered as meanwhile space but instead part of a choreographed strategy to establish place and community.

The need to intensify development on brownfield sites to respond to the housing crisis and evolution of our living and working patterns makes the design of high-quality shared space even more critical. In a world of spreadsheet and regulation led pattern book design it is often the landscape elements of the project that are able most agilely to respond to local specificities to optimize this and in turn maximise opportunities to deliver the social, contextual and commercial value that ensure project viability. Within this context the design of the public realm and place making needs to be reestablished as the critical, fundamental and primary focus, rather than afterthought, of Development in the UK.

BD Landscape Architects' work and process across such a wide range of projects and sectors provide an exemplar of how to achieve this establishing a commercially viable social legacy that will mature and evolve with the planting and landscapes they have delivered.

Andy Puncher is an Architect and Design Director with over 20 years' experience working closely with Developers and Investment Funds delivering medium to large scale projects across London and the Southeast. After 18 years heading up pH+ Architects, which he founded, Andy now works with Developers, Lateral and Fabrix as Design Director on large scale life science and mixed-use led schemes. He is also the UK Development Director for Australian Investment Fund; Solido Capital leading on the acquisition and planning delivery of developments in the UK.

Alongside this Andy is member of the Haringey and Tower Hamlets Quality Review Panels, which he also Chairs. He continues to work with universities in developing and delivering research programmes focussed on delivering sustainable density in complex urban environments.

Andy Puncher *(Design Director, Lateral and Fabrix)*

3 Places for People

Forest Road

"In what can sometimes be a hectic world, it is always encouraging to be involved with projects that allow provision for invaluable space for people to grow their own produce and plants, to help nurture themselves and nature."

Helen Kirk (Senior Associate, BD)

The beautiful Arts and Crafts heritage and the lush greenery of Forest Road in Walthamstow provided rich inspiration with such a strong genius loci. The Pocket Living scheme, completed in 2024, is located opposite the grade II* listed William Morris Gallery and Lloyd Park. Our client Pocket Living – who provide affordable, community-centred homes to allow Londoners to get their feet on the housing ladder – purchased the site to provide 90 one-bedroom apartments for local people.

Our vision was for the landscape to become the heart of the new community; to be flexible and encourage interaction and social time spent outdoors.

The prominent northern side of the site borrows from the established trees along Forest Road, and features a new semi-mature tree plus murals from a local artist inspired by William Morris. The triangular building form picks up on historic street frontages, with materials that follow the vernacular of the local area. This has been extended into the landscape palette through golden-red brick platforms, walls, and matte bronze-coloured angular planters.

The triangular building focuses on a central growing space, which became a key part of our concept, and we were delighted that green-fingered residents quickly took up the opportunity to grow their own vegetables and salads when they moved in. Table tennis and picnic tables also encourage residents outdoors; and ground floor units open onto terraces that connect with the wider courtyard, providing instant ownership and access. Third and fourth floor terraces give residents an opportunity to take in both the sunrise and the sunset.

The soft landscape works hard to bring year-round greening and biodiversity across every level of the scheme. An additional biodiverse 'brown' roof at fourth floor provides opportunity for local flora to pop up and supply pollinators with ruderal habitat; flowering climbing plants subtly divide private terraces; tall grasses, shrubs, and herbs are planted throughout. Five existing strawberry trees onsite were also carefully lifted and relocated within the central courtyard, giving instant impact, year-round interest and continuing the legacy of planting in this green corner of London.

"Over the years collaborating with BD at Pocket and at Hawkins\Brown, we've successfully delivered projects together where landscape enhances the sense of place of the architecture and strengthens social bonds between residents.

Allotments provided give residents a chance to get to know one another, share produce and seek respite from the city. Rooftop terraces celebrate the metropolis in all its guises, and increases social interaction and chance meetings for the residents."

Angharad Palmer ARB, RIBA (Head of Design, Pocket Living)

Forest Road

Riverview Court

Sandwiched between the Upper Bristol Road and the River Avon, Riverview Court is a post-industrial site in the City of Bath's UNESCO World Heritage Site. Lying within Bath's core conservation area; with the adjoining Grade II listed Victoria Bridge and the sensitive ecology of the river; the site presented an exciting – if tricky – series of design challenges to unlock its potential.

Bath & North East Somerset Council envisaged the site as an important node to activate the historic bridge. Rather than doing this through a simple opening-up of the space, our design process focused on an intelligent public realm that enhanced the setting and improved pedestrian and cycle connections.

Working with architects Nash Partnership, the built form proposed a residential led mixed-use pair of buildings with a riverside café. We drew out the landscape to engage meaningfully with the river, as well as linking directly to the Upper Bristol Road and extending the space around the Victoria Bridge to give it valuable breathing space.

Our designs for the river frontage focused on high-quality, warm toned sandstone paving and curving seat-benches to complement the surrounding Bath stone. These catch the sun-filled south-facing aspect and provide informal points to pause and look out across the river, both for new residents and passers-by. Semi-mature tree planting of oaks and amelanchier have provided soft, vertical structure to the riverside; with vertical stands of grasses, sedges, starry alliums, and flowering perennials bring seasonal texture, colour and nectar for pollinators.

The designs enabled us to gain the Council's confidence and promote our client's aim for high-density city centre residences, alongside a striking and biodiverse new piece of public realm leading onto other commissions along the Bath 'River Line'. We hope this sun-filled pocket next to Victoria Bridge will continue to serve as a catalyst for the regeneration of the northern riverside in Bath.

Riverview Court

"A dynamic design that makes imaginative use of a tight space, greatly improves access and enjoyment alongside enhancing historic features."

Society of Landscape & Garden Design Judges

HOLLISTER

Lovedon Fields

Lovedon Fields is a 50-home residential scheme forming a new edge to the village of Kings Worthy, near Winchester in Hampshire. This was a landscape-led project from the very outset: with BD appointed at early concept design stage to work in tandem with John Pardey Architects, and develop a holistic landscape strategy alongside the built form.

The brief from our client HAB [Happiness Architecture Beauty] was 'to make homes that lift the spirits; that are a pleasure to live in and a joy to behold'. Lovedon was part of HAB housing's broader objective to achieve a step-change in the design quality that is expected of and delivered by rural housing developments.

Our design strategy looked to create and maintain a landscape which provides a rich and stimulating environment for residents and visitors, and one that respects the needs and aspirations of the wider community. The landscape was not considered as a cosmetic addition to the environment, but an integrated part of the design, management and function of the development.

From a single point of access from Lovedon Lane, the masterplan for the houses clusters around a triangular open space in the upper part of the site – the Grove. An avenue featuring houses on both sides runs along the lower contours of the site, and re-defines the village edge of Kings Worthy against a generous new semi-natural greenspace of 4.6 hectares. This would act as an extension to the well-used Eversley Park Recreation Ground to the north of our site, which we carefully tied into.

The new parkland was designed as a low key, ecological landscape with an impressive area of native wildflower grassland, criss-crossed by naturalistic footpaths and a running circuit. Allotments, a bike track, and natural play area were designed to gently grade the new development into its countryside setting. Enhanced boundary planting of hedgerow plants and parkland trees also knits the parkland into its local area.

The project as a whole has been designed with local wildlife in mind. New habitats and movement corridors are being created, at varying scales within the park and housing areas; for birds, slow worms, bats, hedgehogs, invertebrates and swifts. Bat boxes, bird boxes and bee bricks are incorporated into the brick walls of the houses. The details of the landscape design were developed to really enhance the sense of home, and encourage interaction and community. Doorstop benches, terraces, calm shared surfaces, and informal meeting spaces all encourage interaction and an instant sense of ownership. Productive growing thresholds were also included to the front boundary of each home, to be planted with edible varieties. These, along with the allotments and planned orchard planting, aimed to encourage residents to participate in gardening and develop a community spirit.

“In marrying the formality of residential development with the freedom of nature it creates the perfect place to live, play and connect. It is beautiful, it is thoughtful… and a time when we urgently need trailblazers in sustainable inhabited landscapes it is hopeful…”

‘Overall Outstanding Winner’ at the 2022 Landscape Institute awards

13

"At HAB we are interested in the edge condition, in sites that occupy the threshold between countryside and town. So many towns and villages have wonderful historic centres but become increasingly anonymous and anodyne towards the settlement edge. Located between Kings Worthy and the South Downs National Park, the Lovedon Lane project offers an opportunity.

The challenge for BD was to design a landscape that mediates between these two different conditions; to reconcile the untamed informality of the open countryside with the intimate domestic spaces which anchor private houses within the public realm. The result is both dense and free; richly-detailed and fine-tuned but also effortless and relaxed; a project that defines the town as being 'of' its glorious rural setting, rather than detached from its surroundings by faceless suburban sprawl."

Isabel Allen (Design Director, HAB Housing)

Lovedon Fields

The public spaces between the homes are multifunctional: offering places to relax, play and socialise whilst also providing hard-working infiltration for periods of extreme rainfall. The diversity of planted species – native hedgerows, shrubs, perennials, bulbs and ecological grassland – also encourage local wildlife as well as seasonal interest for residents. Informal play and social interaction is prominent throughout, with natural play elements, seating and a boules court located within the Grove.

We were over the moon when we got to celebrate Lovedon achieving 'Outstanding Winner' at the 2022 Landscape Institute Awards. This followed both RIBA Regional and RIBA National awards, a shortlisting in the 'Neave Brown Award for Housing', plus a feature in the RIBA publication 'Building in Accordia'. This recognition shows the importance of thoughtful landscape design in residential schemes, and is testament to the creative collaboration and progressive approach central to Lovedon.

"An exemplar of how planning for housing on the edge of an existing settlement should be delivered."

Landscape Institute Judges' comments
Highly commended for 2017 'Local Landscape Planning' award

Earnley Concourse

The pretty village of Earnley lies a short distance from Chichester and Sussex's scenic West Wittering Beach - the Concourse site once being meadow farmland for the local Manor, developed in the mid-20th century as an education institute.

We were delighted to be invited by local housebuilder BRiCS to work with our long-term collaborators John Pardey Architects at Earnley. The Concourse had sadly become derelict and suffered from arson, though the landscape still retained the traces of its original charm through picturesque grassland and mature trees.

We carried out careful studies of the site and its village surroundings, with the aim to create an inspiring environment that respects its natural and rural context, including the neighbouring Medmerry Nature Reserve and the village's conservation area. The masterplan was developed collaboratively to deliver a mix of three to five-bedroom homes set between a rich landscape of woodland meadows, ponds and swales, which will connect strongly to the village and farmland green infrastructure.

A new village green will anchor the north of the Concourse site to its neighbouring historic church and village centre: providing picnic areas, natural play and an orchard copse to engage the new residents in their community. Rills and rain gardens collect water through the streetscape, filtering to swales and ponds to the south. The new streets are carefully designed to minimise large areas of hard standing, with grass-filled permeable paving providing flexibility of access and a tight-knit village feel.

The overgrown field behind the Manor will be enhanced into a generous area of parkland, with the existing mature tree canopy playing host to playful trails, dappled meadows and a looping footpath.

We were really pleased to hear Chichester's Design Officer's comments that "the design approach enables the development to establish its own character and identity...The agricultural references, bold but traditional material palette and high-quality landscape ensure the development relates well to its surroundings". We were very pleased to receive planning consent in 2025, and are looking forward to being involved in the next stages of this beautiful site.

1

2

West Green Place

West Green Place is a verdant new street set beside Downhills Park in the London Borough of Haringey. Another scheme for our client Pocket Living, champions of affordable London starter homes: they asked us to create an inspiring landscape that would bring together new residents and the existing community.

The Dyvik Kahlen-designed Community Centre and Nursery provides a gateway to the site, and a key concept was for our exemplary, pedestrian-focused streetscape to connect those walking and cycling here to Downhills Park. The landscape also aims to create a meaningful transition between its two neighbouring character areas: the tree-filled greenery of the park to the west, and pleasing regularity of Victorian terraces to the east.

The new homes designed by HTA Design provide 126 new residences, of which 78% would be affordable housing featuring communal terraces and facilities, alongside 16 contemporary townhouses with private rear gardens.

The landscape design has created a lush green setting for the new built form, interwoven with features that invite the community in. These include a small urban orchard; food growing pockets; plus a communal square allowing space for people to stretch, play, and hold events alongside the Community Centre.

Soft landscape areas are connected where possible throughout the site to provide green corridors for wildlife, reduce surface water run-off and help cool the landscape during hot summers. Planted with trees, biodiverse shrubs, perennials and bulbs, playful boulders pepper the greenspace to encourage play on the way, and chunky planters provide additional communal growing space.

The scheme has been a great success: a new green corridor providing links for local pollinators, insects, and amphibians to set out beyond Downhills Park. The park's new pedestrian access has also been a triumph, and the streetscape continues to serve as a successful walkable link for the new scheme and their West Green neighbours.

Higher Trannack

> "Higher Trannack is the steeply sloping side of the Chyandour valley immediately north of Penzance. The challenging terrain resulted in a terraced masterplan of dwellings and spaces that enjoy extraordinary southerly views across Mounts Bay and Penzance."

John Pardey Architects

On the Chyandour valley's steep northern side lies Trannack Farm, just above Penzance and overlooking the sublime scenery of the town, St Michael's Mount and Mounts Bay. Devonshire Homes asked BD and our long-standing collaborators John Pardey Architects to imagine a 320-home design for this allocated site, and make the most of the extraordinary views.

The challenging terrain gave our team a richly terraced masterplan of dwellings and public open spaces. By making the most of each plateau and slope we were able to work closely with the topography to retain the special character of the site, including its old 'drangs' – a Cornish word for narrow lanes.

Throughout the masterplan we designed a variety of natural 'lingering spaces' for people to play, socialise, walk, and watch the seascape change around St.Michael's Mount. In all there is an impressive 9.4 hectares of public open space: new community allotments; an orchard for local apple varieties; Great Hill and Long Meadow nature trail; wet woodlands and sustainable drainage ponds.

A key piece of the landscape design is for a central communal gathering and play place inspired by the Cornish 'Plen an Gwari' tradition, medieval amphitheatres where local people would have performed plays. This proved a very popular idea amongst local residents during the public engagement, which was hugely important for us during the sketching out of the public landscape.

The historic patterns, flora and fauna of this corner of Cornwall really inspired us to design a landscape that celebrates local identity and character. Higher Trannack received planning in 2024, and we are looking forward to seeing this special site begin to take shape in the near future.

Playful Places

by Carl Gulland (Director, John Pardey Architects)

This morning, I cycled to work. Realising I had forgotten my laptop I cycled straight home and then back. Six and a half miles had become nineteen and a half and apart from a fleeting moment of irritation my day was all the better for it – my involuntary smile seen by the people I passed and bullfinches in the hedgerows. Sure, dopamine was released and muscles warmed but between glimpses of a hare, an unidentified bird of prey, deer cautious at a woodland edge was space to be in the moment and space for thoughts to emerge and settle. I cycle most days; I have chosen to live close enough to work and amenities that cycling is always an option and only the very worst weather a deterrent. My first bike, found under the Christmas tree, ridden with glee to the old railway embankment – a haven of crickets; to Kevin's house to look at his football cards; in convoy with the other neighbourhood children. That first bike and all the subsequent bikes and the expanding horizons that age and adventure encouraged cemented the potential of the bike to bring low-cost freedom – the wind in my hair, the open road, the open mind and the healthy body that at 54 I increasingly appreciate.

A career in architecture perhaps sparked by moving into one of the first houses on Heron Gate – an ornithologically inspired but otherwise non-descript Seventies housing estate. Health and Safety not yet a thing meant free run of part finished houses and ready access to den building materials. Parents oblivious to risks being taken apart from the occasional request for a plaster. Generally, I was sent back out with a ball of cottonwool doused with Witch-hazel.
At dawn tomorrow I'll check the surfcam at Bournemouth Pier to see if the 'Poor to Fair' forecast on Surfline has manifested then hopefully head to the beach to ride waves and get that very same thrill that the 8-year-old me did on my penny skateboard down the smooth tarmac path parallel to Stokesley Road. A five-minute walk to the top rewarded by a 50 second ride. The one-inch scar where I skidded on my left hip bone is still visible as are a multitude of others – each with a story, each thanks to play.

Legs brace as I dive my red Peter Powell Stunt Kite on The Green, West Parade, Criccieth – a summer holiday present and a danger to any passing car or pedestrian. Saturday just gone and I felt the same exhilaration of converting wind to speed on my windsurfing kit. Like living cycling distance to work, I've engineered a lifestyle that has kept open the forms of play I love.

The evening the police knocked on the door at Bredero Drive, Banchory. A neighbour had complained about my brother and I playing tennis in the street – re-enacting the 1980 Borg McEnroe final. Tennis has been a sporadic part of my life since. My brother plays weekly and can still impersonate the serves of all the greats.

1981 was the summer of tree climbing. Wild cherry trees (Geans) dressed the banks of the River Dee, and every day of the school holiday was an opportunity for Mark Saunders and me to climb, scoff cherries and whittle branches with sheath knives on our belts and the occasional unplanned fall onto bank or into river - part and parcel of the expanded horizon of a 10-year-old.
Anecdotes from a childhood of outdoor play that are vivid in my memory and could be multiplied ten times over. Each a vital component in a continuum of play that has kept me young and more or less sane. Many of our memories of childhood are entwined with being outdoors – a given, right? And yet the data tell us this universal and timeless truth is severely under threat.

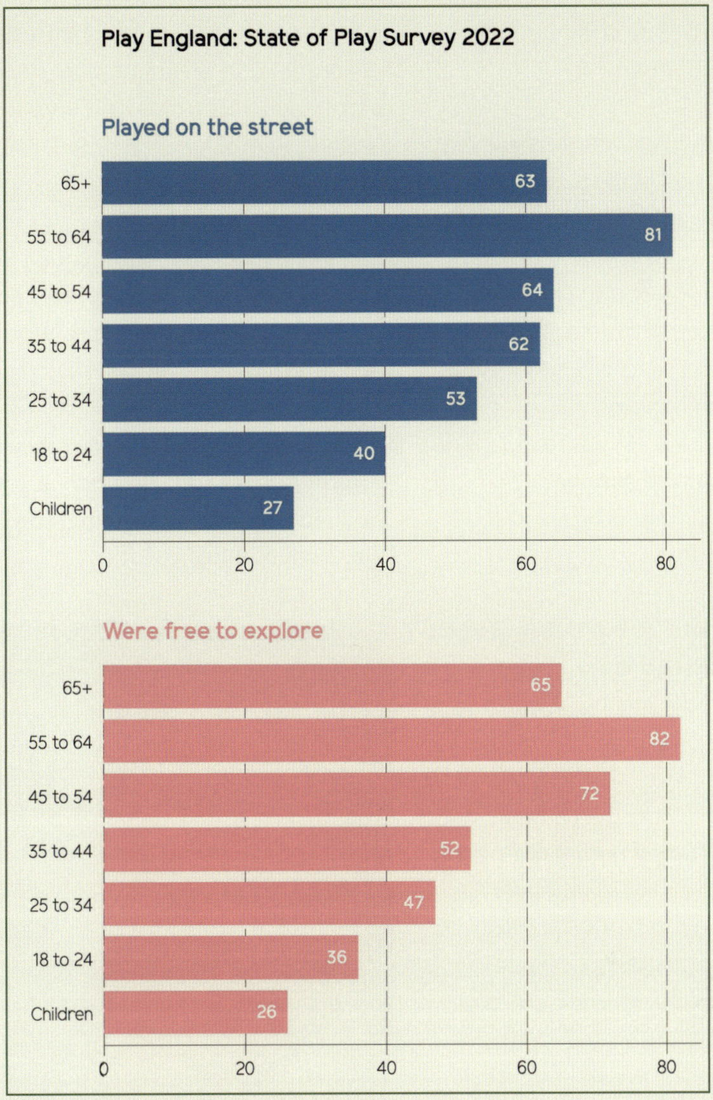

Is my love song to play turning into eulogy? My recipe for physical, mental and spiritual well-being flagging-up a health warning? My visceral experiences replaced with virtual thrills?

Researchers, think-tanks, provocateurs and politicians are all prophesying and proposing how this plays out. As an architect my opportunities to influence and impact are project by project and by creating a built backdrop that my landscape collaborators can stage shared spaces. And there is no more joyous collaboration than those I have had with Rob and his team at BD – because joy and delight is what they bring in spades. Together we have created playful places.

Jim Stephenson filmed our project at Lovedon Fields over a few days and incorporating the annual summer street party. Children run into a maze in the tall grasses of the attenuation swale. A mum and 3 young daughters walking, skipping down the middle of the road dispensing with the pavements that Hampshire Highways felt were indispensable. And the squared off oak trunks that are scattered across the scheme: as suitable as a base for a game of hide and seek as they are a bench to share a glass of wine of an evening.

Playful places encourage play. Good landscape design at a fraction of the cost of buildings can transform the potential of new and existing spaces to be active spaces – spaces where people choose to hang out, young and old. Places where people want to live. Places with a sense of community. Places with an actual community.

Playful places change priorities – a streetscape that is engaging and usable by all is also a streetscape where drivers snap out of autopilot and expect the unexpected.

Playful places make getting places fun. Benches, logs, banks, rocks, flowers, water all engage senses, create pauses, encourage meeting.

Playful places knit habitat and rainwater management, soft and hard surfaces into a whole that is greater than the parts.

Playful places allow horizons to grow, they connect visually and physically to the context. Those connections also welcome in and build wider community.

Can playful places buck the trend for a homeward retreat and a diminished neighbourhood? Perhaps. The homes we build today need significantly less energy to stay warm than the 1970s equivalent. Landscape design and placemaking in the housing estates of my childhood seems now like an afterthought but that didn't matter so much - the street and garden was still where I found fun without the distractions of phones let alone much in the way of children's TV. My guess is that the spaces between buildings need to work much harder now to draw our children from virtual worlds into a truly immersive environment. Just as homes have become more comfortable, the spaces between need to become a more comfortable place to hang-out. This requires the sort of landscape designers that BD are – practical, colourful, resourceful, playful.

As a hopeful footnote, the proposal for Lovedon Fields included a BMX track identified in consultation with local schools. While 10 years on the Council have finally delivered the allotments, the BMX track is still awaited but undeterred local young people have created their own on an adjacent piece of open ground – if you want to check out the action look at the YouTube page of 'Bro's with nothing to do'!

Image: Kings Worthy Bike Park
– created by young people for young people!

Carl is a director of John Pardey Architects. Based in the New Forest, the practice has designed houses across the UK often in extraordinary and sensitive places. Carl leads on housing and placemaking including Lovedon Fields outside Winchester which as well as RIBA and Landscape Institute Awards was recently recognised locally by the Winchester City Trust.

A formative project for Carl was Accordia, Cambridge when he was at Feilden Clegg Bradley Studios. Twenty years old, Accordia is a project that changed the conversation about housing and placemaking prioritising shared landscapes that benefit young and are fundamental for nurturing a sense of community.

4

The Biophilic Campus

RAU Innovation Village

The Royal Agricultural University's Cirencester campus is the planned home of the groundbreaking ten hectare RAU Innovation Village. This landscape-led reimagining of the existing campus will really push the boundaries of sustainable design – providing a new hub for agricultural, food, and land management entrepreneurs and researchers, amongst a nature-rich landscape. Our brief has been to design a place that is beautiful, carbon neutral, biodiversity rich and inspires innovation through its environment.

The Cirencester campus lies at the edge of the designated Cotswold National Landscape; set amongst mature parkland trees. The remnants of historic ridge and furrow field patterns and the culturally significant University built form provided us with a strong heritage to carefully weave our designs through. These elements all underpinned our landscape strategy, developed in collaboration with the RAU and Passivhaus experts Architype.

Our initial concepts included reducing the dominance of vehicles onsite; teasing out the many landmark trees and buildings to improve their setting; preserving and enhancing the site's extensive grassland for biodiversity; and improving wildlife connections through enhanced, joined-up habitats.

The heart of our design's sustainability credentials are its nature-based solutions. As well as the connected green infrastructure of pathways and linear ecosystems - connecting both wildlife and the RAU's future inhabitants to all parts of the campus, the sustainable drainage design responds sensitively to the site's subtle topography and existing character. We believe the energy of the heightened seasonal changes and new biodiversity will help to encourage people into their landscape, stir their senses, and inspire creating thinking.

We really enjoyed engaging with stakeholders and the agricultural industry throughout the design process, with the project submitted for outline planning approval in March 2024. We can't wait to see the Innovation Village start to take shape in the near future, and be filled with new habitats, wildlife and innovators!

ARK EdCity

EdCity, located in the White City Estate is a not-for-profit partnership between national education charity Ark and Hammersmith & Fulham Council. As an education charity, Ark's aim is to ensure that children across all backgrounds have access to excellent education. They asked BD to be part of the team transforming the site, into a multifacility community hub and the jewel of their estate.

Our designs for the landscape look to create a vibrant, flexible public realm to unite the diverse mix of groups proposed for the site. Our process was driven by stakeholder engagement with the school, the youth zone operator, the nursery, and local residents and community centres within the estate – as well as Ark themselves. This engagement focused our vision for landscape spaces to encourage people of all backgrounds and ages to socialise, learn, and play together in a safe, healthy and enriching environment.

The central element of our public realm design has been a linear, pedestrianised, boulevard which weaves together the different volumes. A huge range of mature tree planting, including ten-metre tall London planes, pines, and umbrella-form birches, look over ornamental and flower-rich raingardens; opening the site up to the surrounding estate. The final landscape scheme will create a vibrant public realm that unites the diverse mix of stakeholders proposed for the site. It will provide spaces for people of all backgrounds and ages to socialise, learn and play together in a safe, healthy and enriching environment.

Phase one of the project was finished in 2024 and already looks lush and verdant, covering the Ark Swift Primary School, new Ark headquarters and sports zone. Phase two is well under way and due for completion in 2025, to include; Harmony Nursery, Adult Community Education Centre alongside affordable housing for local people.

ARK EdCity

Step!
Jump!
WEST

This expansive scheme that we have been working on for well over a decade is split over five volumes across multiple phases with a variety of end users and stakeholders. It has been a real challenge and the strong design team relationships have helped to shape the final proposals. I am looking forward to seeing the planting, in particular, establish over the coming years to create a strong green thread through the site; in line with our original design intent from back in 2016!

Emma Santamaria (Senior Associate, BD)

Fidelity Campus

Fidelity International's largest UK office at Kingswood Fields is set within Surrey's rolling green belt, and surrounded by Ancient Woodland. As part of Fidelity's plans to accommodate extra staff, BD were appointed to consider a site-wide regeneration for the thriving campus – already home to a raft of their business. This includes technology, marketing, customer services and finance departments; an onsite deli and restaurant; gym, plus running clubs and campus walking routes.

Our brief focused on developing a fluid and contemporary setting across the masterplan, facilitating connections and interactions through a thriving heart – alongside a radical enhancement in biodiversity. We have so far worked on three key spaces for Fidelity: the Heart Zone; Pavilion; and a redesign of their core parking facilities.

The Heart Zone project has delivered the thriving new core required for the campus. The branching, irregular space includes the Gateway Plaza and links the three main buildings onsite: Beech Gate House, Kingswood Place and Windmill Court.

Our key design ambitions were:

- To create a healthy, joyful, green heart that inspires employees during their daily work.
- To frame and enhance the views of the red brick architecture.
- To optimise the function and flow of people by providing clear and joined-up routes and clever signage.
- To foster community and interaction through social spaces.
- We wanted to achieve all of the above through the principles of 'biophilic design': bringing the natural world into our design to improve human wellbeing.

Our vision was to enrich the heart of the site through a series of design highlights reminiscent of natural landscapes: river, meadow, mountain, woodland. As such, our initial designs started to draw in elements of rain gardens, open courtyard, incidental seating, naturalistic ornamental planting, and edible landscape pockets.

We also wanted the Heart Zone to feel coherent, connected and improve navigation throughout the wider site. An important aspect was therefore the rationalisation of levels to seamlessly link the buildings and avoid steps wherever possible to improve flow and accessibility. Careful consideration to the sequence of arrival from the Gateway Plaza to the reception entrance was also a key consideration for us.

Surface profiles and details have been designed to direct surface water runoff into a central rain garden that wraps around the Kingswood building. Planted with damp-tolerant plants and encompassed by amphitheatre seating, this focal point ensures a visually attractive and hardworking, multi-functional landscape. Permeable paving to drop-off areas also absorbs surface water as part of the sustainable drainage strategy.

Our soft landscape designs create a green oasis at the heart of the campus. As part of our biophilic approach, the design has incorporated a variety of species-rich habitats – including dappled shady woodland, wildflower meadow, and flood-able landscape. Together these create an attractive and sensory-rich workplace setting, which is constantly growing and changing with year-round visual interest. This promotes people's wellbeing and connection to nature, as well as combining and enhancing the site's existing biodiversity.
Heart Zone won the 2022 Landscape Institute Award for 'Excellence in Horticulture and Planting Design', and features tall, swaying stands of grasses that turn blond in autumn; herbs and shrubby structure; plus spring to autumn-flowering colourful perennials to extend the season for pollinators.

Our work also proposed a number of feature trees throughout the site: semi-mature ornamental trees; fruiting orchard trees; and specimen screening trees. This tree network defines the spaces and contributes to the sequence of arrival, directs key views, and provides year-round structure.

We have thoroughly enjoyed working on the masterplan and three projects across Fidelity's campus: contributing to the successful planning applications, technical design and overseeing the landscape construction works on site.

"The spaces provide an enticing environment for employees to take a break, relax and socialise. The provision of these lush green spaces will certainly have an impact on the users health and wellbeing."

Landscape Institute Judges' comments
Overall Winner for 2022 'Excellence in Horticulture + Planting Design'

Fidelity Campus

"The heart space is looking beautiful."

Christopher O'Connell (Site Supervisor - CBRE)

Fidelity Campus

Project Cross

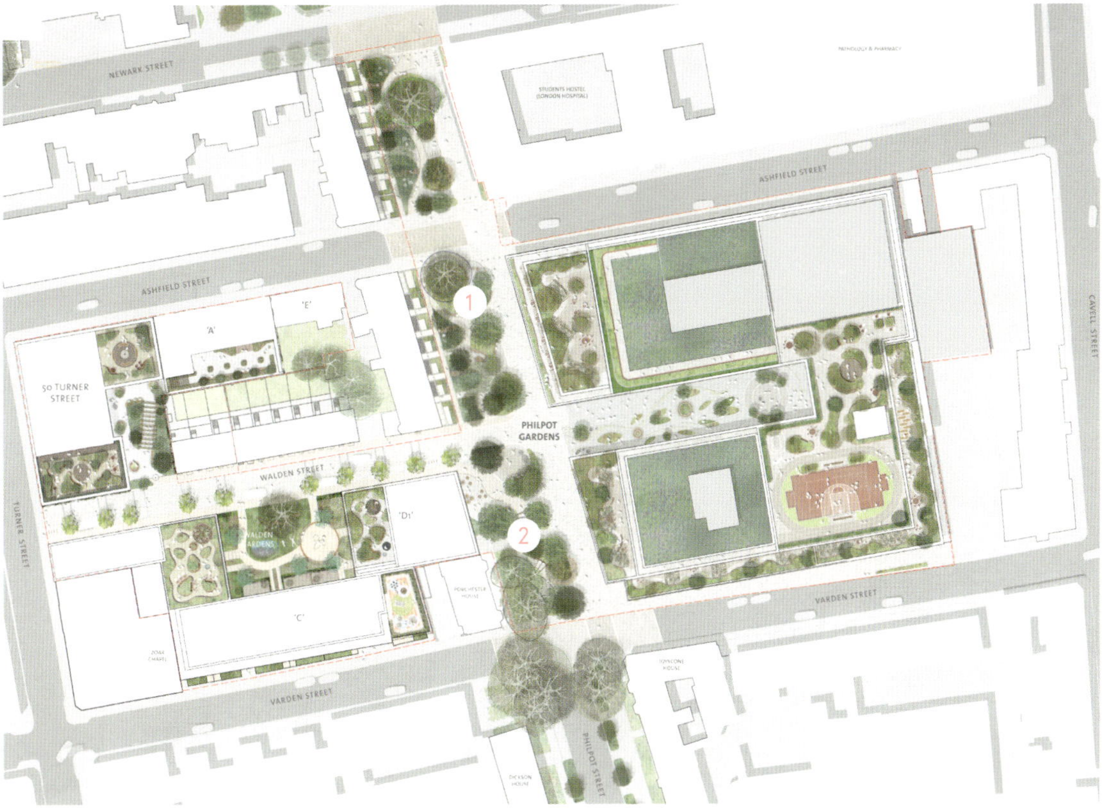

BD have been collaborating with PLP Architecture, DSDHA, dmfk and client Bentall Green Oak on the transformation of the Whitechapel Estate. The team's brief is to deliver world-class life science buildings and NHS key worker housing, set amongst enhanced public spaces.

The Whitechapel Estate encompasses the land between Varden Street and Ashfield Street, and will become home to a complex of 13 different buildings. The eastern half will feature an array of lab, office and storage spaces; with the western half including new residences for those working within the NHS, plus extra for market sale.

60,000 square metres of life-science-enabled space will significantly contribute to wider plans for the development of a Whitechapel Life Science Campus; of which over 15% will be pre-let to the Barts Health NHS Trust.

Our designs set out a vital green heart at Mulberry Gardens – inspired by the site's rich, layered history – alongside the wider public realm improvements which envisage a healing landscape for all. The landscape will encourage contact with nature and transform the existing public realm into a series of restorative green spaces connected together through a linear 'green spine'.

The improved natural surveillance intrinsic to the scheme will provide safe and welcoming spaces that support residents, staff and patients with their health and wellbeing, alongside tackling anti-social behaviour. Our designs retain the key trees as part of the green spine, woven through layers of biophilic, healing planting. Sustainable drainage and tactile natural play are also interlaced to make a truly multi-functional place, engaged with the healing powers of natural processes.

The roof terraces also include over 3,500 square metres of biodiverse living roofs, including a communal 1,700 square metre terrace open to key workers – with chances to socialise, rest and be amongst rooftop greenery to support their wellbeing.

The scheme was submitted for planning in 2025 and we are excited to see its next steps.

Reflections on Transforming Urban Sites: A Developer's Perspective on Landscape and Public Realm

by Steve Sanham (Director, Common Projects)

As we prepare for a decade of intensified development across the UK, focussed especially on brownfield sites, it's critical that developers, housebuilders and planners appreciate the importance of landscape – the foundation of successful places and a key creator of value, resilience and wellbeing. If we are serious about harnessing development's power to change cities by creating lasting, healthy, and inclusive places, then landscape must be considered core infrastructure: designed skilfully, delivered early, and maintained well. Our approach to landscape in fact inspired our business name: Common, meaning a public space 'owned by everyone', existing for shared benefit, planned for the long-term.

One of the most significant mindset shifts among developers in the past decade is the growing recognition that landscape is no longer a decorative afterthought, but essential infrastructure, both environmental and human. Whether offering shade in a heatwave, supporting mental health in a high-pressure society, or providing space for communities to gather, landscape is a public good with far-reaching value.

This means we must think differently about how we plan, design and invest in the creation, and ongoing management, of public realm. Landscape should not be squeezed into leftover space, 'value engineered' at the eleventh hour, or treated as a planning requirement to be ticked off. Instead, it should be integral to the DNA of any new development – on a par with buildings, transport, and utilities. The King's Cross masterplan took the Nolli principle of setting out the public realm first, marking the important plazas, streets and gardens that form the 'skeleton' of an urban neighbourhood. If these work, the buildings will follow. If they don't, places feel cramped, confusing, not at human scale. Widths of streets, their curves, clever sightlines from one to another that create unexpected glimpses of green, blue, heritage – these are all small considerations with enormous impact. The best landscape designers feel this instinctively and deliver it precisely.

Done properly, then, landscape becomes the spatial logic of a place. It shapes how people navigate neighbourhoods, where they pause, what they remember, how they can connect. It plays a critical role in fostering community. Inviting, shared public spaces offer 'neutral ground' – places where different groups can interact informally and safely. A treasured public space feels like it doesn't belong to just anyone – but it does feel like it belongs to everyone.

We don't always talk enough about how landscape affects people, but the evidence is there. It's intuitive – part of being human? – that exposure to green environments reduces stress, anxiety and depression. Even brief interactions with nature, like taking a detour through a pocket park, choosing to pause near a water feature, or simply seeing greenery from a window, produce measurable psychological benefits.

This is not soft stuff. It's exactly the kind of resilience we should be designing for in the face of mounting public health pressure, climate volatility, and social fragmentation. King's Cross, again, serves as an example. Events, performances, markets and casual encounters all unfold against a carefully thought out green backdrop. These are not just "nice places" – they are really important contributors to wellbeing, identity, and urban life. From a development perspective, investing in good landscape also makes commercial sense. Well-designed public realm can increase dwell time, improve footfall, and attract tenants. Well-maintained, it supports longer-term asset performance, and strengthens a place's 'brand' identity.

Critically, it lasts. Built assets will be extended, relet, reclad, and in some cases demolished. But public realm, when it's done right, endures, and becomes part of the 'mental map' of a city. Working on urban landscape is not a separate design meeting! It's part of the ongoing development agenda. Too often, public realm ambitions are retrofitted into a design that has already fixed the costly decisions - basement layouts, levels, materials. At that stage, most of the opportunity is lost.

Looking ahead to what projects like Wandsworth Gasworks can learn from places like King's Cross (both projects we have worked on), embedding landscape early in the design process is non-negotiable. Also a former industrial site, also defined for decades by gas holders and hard infrastructure, it is being reimagined as a mixed-use district with public realm one of its defining elements. Green infrastructure will not be the residual space between buildings, but the structural 'backbone' of the development. The green 'Gasholder Way' running through the site, along with the Wandle Trail, connects blocks and buildings to pocket parks, community spaces and open riverfront.

Movement, nature, and people are being planned all-together. Landscape is shared space, and in many ways defines whether a place works. Your public will never enter the majority of buildings you deliver – but they will experience, and hopefully love, your public realm. People notice landscape! The seasonality of planting, the sound of nearby water, the way trees line a boulevard, the quality of street furniture. These are choices whose impacts may be hard to measure, but because they're emotional ones, they are lasting.

The transformation of brownfield sites like King's Cross shows that bold, upfront investment in landscape can turn underused urban land into a place that feels purposeful, inviting, valuable. As Wandsworth Gasworks moves forward, it has the opportunity to do the same.

We need to approach landscape with the same rigour and intentionality as any piece of engineering or architecture. That means early investment, integrated thinking, and a long view on quality. If we get it wrong, no amount of good architecture can save it.

Common Projects, founded by Steve Sanham in 2021, funds and delivers complex and game-changing development projects, drawing on decades of combined experience and a desire to champion positive change in development. Its current projects include Zodiac and the redevelopment of Wandsworth Gasworks.

Its approach is underpinned by research and analysis, rooted in financial, technical and practical competence, and delivered with purpose. Common Projects uses the skills inherent in successful property development to address, mitigate or reverse issues caused by the sector; its transformational work delivers community empowerment, homes for those most in need, bold responses to the climate emergency, and support for the arts and culture our cities must protect.

5 Destination Landscape

Tides Reach

"Salcombe in Devon is now home to what could be the coolest beach club in the UK."

The Times

A little further down the coast from chapter one's The Strand: the Harbour Beach Club is a new boutique hotel and spa in the South Devon National Landscape, overlooking the golden sands and green coast of the Salcombe Estuary.

The plans made the most of the building's unique beachside location overlooking South Sands cove, with a 44-bedroom boutique hotel proposed, alongside adaptive reuse of the original 1930s building into ten luxury waterfront apartments. The plans also comprised a restaurant, bar, and chic spa, all enhanced by the landscape of sunny dining terraces and beachy promenades, blending seamlessly with the natural environment.

Our landscape designs also focused on enhancing the large pond, fed by a local stream, and contributing to the on site sustainable drainage strategy. We wanted to bring echoes of Slapton Ley National Nature Reserve – a nearby natural freshwater lake intertwined with reeds, marsh and wet woodland; as well as the rugged dune habitats of Slapton Sands. Structural grasses along pond and raingarden edges provide a visual buffer as the ground drops away, with pockets of raised planting for dry-habitat planting – ensuring colour and interest during all seasons.

The masterplan also incorporated raised `floating' terraces, designed to provide compensatory floodwater storage during storm events and sensitively incorporated with welcoming stepped and lift access to the hotel's main entrance.

The project received planning permission in 2016 thanks to the sympathetic designs which responded to the sensitivities of the National Landscape (formerly known as the AONB), the constrained site, and neighbours such the nearby National Trust's Overbecks Garden.

Tides Reach

Stadium for Bath

We are delighted to be working on the landscape designs for the proposed 18,000 seat stadium in the UNESCO World Heritage City of Bath – an enhanced destination for events, and an improved home for Bath Rugby. The site comprises the smaller, existing stadium and lies in the heart of the historic city next to the River Avon, adjacent to Pulteney Bridge and weir.

The new facility will replace the existing rugby stadium, and provide a welcoming and considered venue set in this iconic riverside setting. From the outset, BD's landscape vision has sought to celebrate this unique setting; enhance the flow and visitor experience to encourage people's active travel to the site; and reintroduce the concept of a pleasure garden and social destination. These concepts have all run alongside our previous experience of working with B&NES Council's Waterspace Guidance, which sets out lighting constraints and parameters to ensure a consistent, ecological approach for the World Heritage city.

We have worked closely with Kay Elliott architects to ensure the designs respond sensitively to the important heritage setting. In addition to providing a significantly improved facility for sports and events, the scheme delivers new public realm right beside the river by moving the stadium slightly further from the River Avon, providing opportunities for a variety of circulation and dwelling spaces along the riverside, including the new Riverside Gate arrival space.

Our designs for the landscape detail reflect the rich historic and cultural heritage, from the site's previous use as a Victorian pleasure garden to its recent history as a world-renowned rugby club. These will include high quality paved surfacing and street furniture, alongside a soft landscape strategy which retains the network of riverside trees, underplanted with shade-loving perennials and bulbs that create the new 'Spring Walk'.

The designs were submitted for planning in late 2024, and BD's rugby fans can't wait to see the project progress.

"Any new development in the heart of Bath will always come with its unique challenges. That's what keeps it interesting, but ultimately rewarding."

Guto Jones (Senior Associate, BD)

2

Pulteney Bridge
Beazer Maze
Pulteney Weir
2
Grand Parade
River Avon
Bath Rugby Football Club
The Recreation Ground
1
Bath Sports and Leisure Centre
Parade Gardens
North Parade Bridge

Heal's

Heal's is a historic furniture and homeware store for world-class design, and has operated from its Tottenham Court Road base in Fitzrovia since 1840. BD were asked to reimagine Alfred Mews which it bounds to the south, as well as a roof terrace and internal courtyard. This was a constrained landscape with big ambitions.

The intention for these reimagined spaces was to enhance the visitor experience and connect with the historic built form. As Heal's was founded within the manufacturing industry, specifically mattresses and later furniture, we looked at historic images of these processes to draw inspiration. Makers' feather baskets provided us with forms for bespoke raised planters, with related designs for seating inspired by manufacturer's workbenches. A series of 'light touch' and long-term design sketches for Alfred Mews will be used by Heal's as their masterplan continues. These neatly combine the constraints around maintenance vehicle access with an exciting opportunity for restaurant spill-out space, lush greening, and a natural stone material palette to enhance the Mews' setting.

Our linked designs for the landscape terrace provides office amenity space with dining areas, planted pergola shelters, and flexible spaces for people to chat and unwind. The pergolas provide an opportunity for sheltered 'outdoor rooms' and create a sense of privacy and enclosure. Their evergreen climbing plants filter views out in this high-density spot, as well as providing habitat structure and flowers for biodiversity.

Our materials and colour selection have tied carefully into the architectural palette, as well as to other nearby terrace schemes, in order to create a sense of continuity between external spaces. We chose an ornamental mix of drought-tolerant planting with an oriental theme, to suit the architectural setting. BD took the scheme from concept design through to completion in 2024.

Heal's

The Liberty – Romford

1

2

BD have been working on the large-scale urban regeneration of the Liberty shopping centre and surrounding public realm through 2025 with an award-winning design team including SHEDkm for developers HUB.

The Romford Masterplan, adopted by Havering Council, sets out a bold and comprehensive vision for Romford Town Centre – placing The Liberty at its heart. Against the backdrop of the historic centre of town, our proposals to create a vibrant and thriving destination for eating, socialising and living will be key to realising that vision.

We are preparing a hybrid planning application for three plots at the Liberty – each designed to revitalise the centre and its links to the wider town centre. We are reimagining the heart of Romford to be greener, easier to navigate, and more welcoming for everyone with increased areas of public realm.

Our landscape masterplan includes improved connections, vibrant gateways, and flexible, inviting spaces for people to enjoy.

New public areas will offer places to sit, play, or pause—enhanced with trees, planting, lighting, and features that make the space feel safer and more attractive. Better routes to the Marketplace, clearer signage, and space for events and popups will help draw people in and encourage them to return.

These improvements of will be made possible through new housing including circa 650 BTR units.

After introducing our early vision in May 2025 and our emerging proposals in July, we're now taking time to prepare our detailed designs and ensure they are an evolution of what already makes Romford a great place to live, work, and spend time with planning aiming to be submitted towards the end of 2025.

Living Wetland Theatre

This one-of-a-kind project provides an open air venue for interactive talks and live bird flight demonstrations on stage: the Living Wetland Theatre and adjacent Waterscapes Aviary. The project formed part of a £4.4million National Lottery Heritage Fund awarded to the Wildfowl & Wetlands Trust's (WWT) Slimbridge Wetland Centre in Gloucestershire. The WWT are the wetland restoration charity, and we are proud to be part of their incredible work in conservation and education.

The basis for the Living Wetland Theatre is that 'wetlands are amazing!' – yet these amazing places are under threat of being lost. In line with the WWT's values, a new waterscapes aviary exhibit to celebrate the diversity of UK wetlands – and teach people about their restoration – was envisaged at Slimbridge. This could feature reedbeds, marsh and tidal estuarine environments, and house a whole host of native bird species from small passerines – bearded reedling, reed warbler – to graceful waders, ducks, little egrets and spoonbills.

Our initial work included in-depth desktop study and site visits through the year to experience the existing site, its topography, existing landscape features and its microclimate within context of the wider wetlands site, which lies close to the River Severn. These layers of information informed our development of the site's layout options, which we worked through closely alongside Kay Elliott Architects, Hoare Lea, and David Dexter Engineers. The exhibit's developing design was honed in close collaboration with WWT, and we kept Slimbridge's thousands of visitors, dedicated staff, and its wildlife in mind throughout. The Waterscapes Aviary had to be home to a variety of bird species 365 days of the year; be accessible to all for an enriched educational experience; and an immersive sensory experience. To achieve the latter, the sound of birds would be paired with our vision for textured planting, changing as you transition through the aviary. Talks and demonstrations would be provided in a new amphitheatre space, bringing the experience to life. Thought also had to be given to the practicalities of diverting a watercourse through the site, as well as the day-to-day site servicing, management of the birds and the habitats.

The finished scheme highlights the valuable habitat that wetlands provide and their diverse flora and fauna. The entrance gives views to an enticing, intimate amphitheatre, which visitors reach by crossing a stream bridge, and where they can watch wonders such as Sprout the pink-backed pelican taking flight. After the demonstration, visitors can take a meandering route through the aviary and catch views of native birds enjoying freshwater pools, sandy shores, reedbeds and mud flats.

The 360-seat Living Theatre features a winged shelter to help protect from the elements, and had to be high enough to enable birds to fly from the back of the tiered seating to the stage. The rainwater collected from its roof feeds into the watercourse feeding the aviary wetland as a sustainable drainage feature. Reclaimed timber groynes have been installed to create an authentic backdrop to the stage, and house the large screen. Their use is also repeated throughout the aviary as part of the signage strategy.

Living Wetland Theatre
Garfield Weston Foundation

"The scheme's execution is a remarkable journey, seamlessly transitioning from initial design to intricate construction."

Landscape Institute Judges' comments
Highly commended for 2023 'Excellence in Small Landscape Design' award

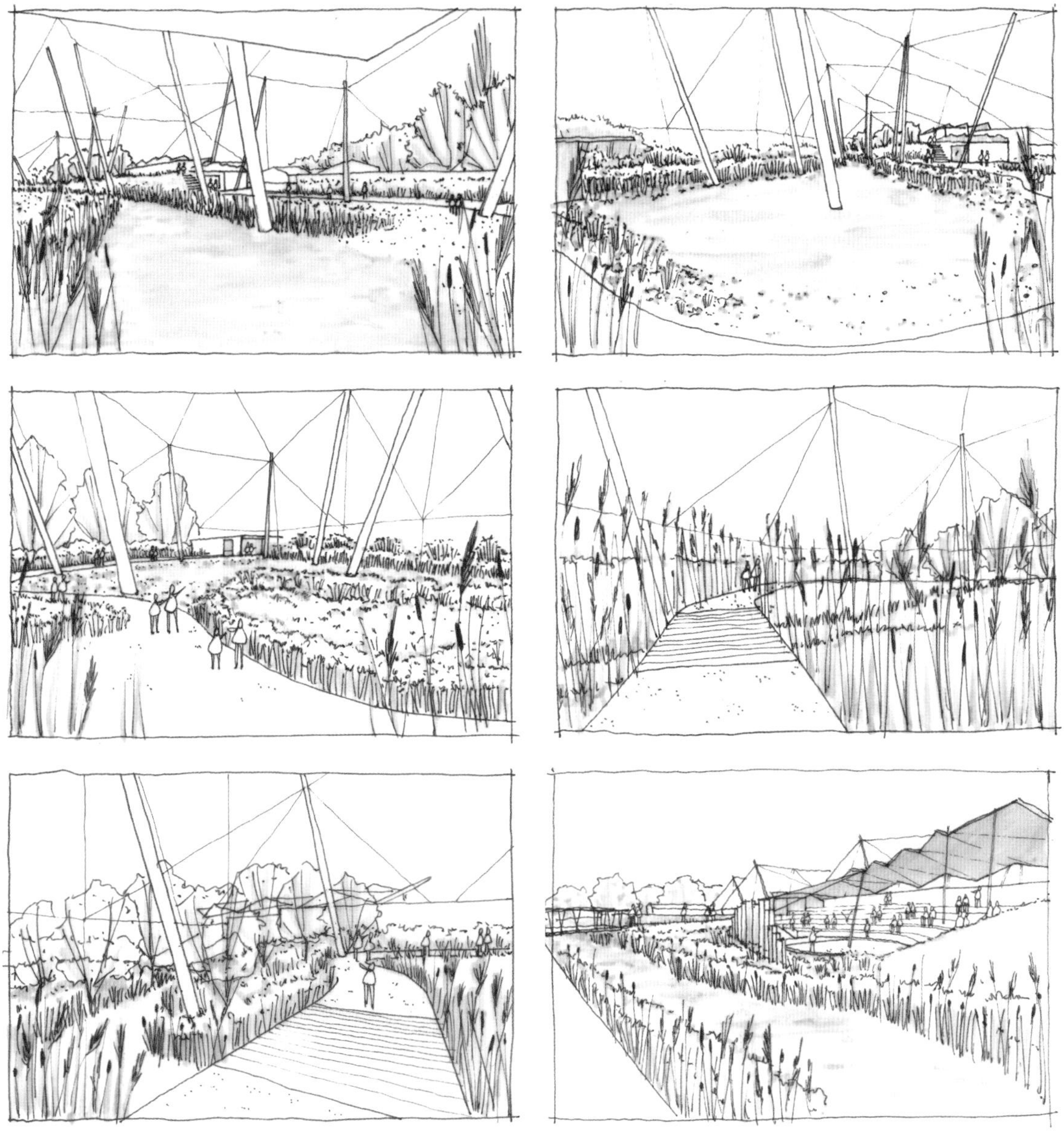

Hard landscape materials were selected to sympathetically provide even and stable routes as part of the accessibility strategy. It was important to allow easy movement from the amphitheatre through the sloping landscape of the aviary, whilst still providing a naturalistic landscape. Our design therefore features a winding path from the entrance, through the Living Wetland Theatre, and on through the aviary at accessible gradients. Bridges provide routes across streams, and a chance for visitors to experience the water close up.

The Waterscapes Aviary saw the creation of a new lagoon, fed from a new stream which connects to Slimbridge's wider wetland network. This provides a connected, robust and rich natural habitat for wetland invertebrates, and forms the key habitat base for the aviary's birds. An immersive environment for visitors has therefore been created, with the sights and sounds of a British wetland – here people can look out for bearded reedlings, watch diving ducks in the underwater duck tank, and learn about butterflies, dragonflies and pond creatures that rely on wetlands for their survival.

The habitats are planted to showcase the plant biodiversity of UK wetland species matrices. Our soft landscape designs therefore comprise a variety of native trees, wildflowers, reed and aquatic planting, providing many opportunities for wildlife to find natural places to perch, nest and shelter.

Living Wetland Theatre

WWT were pleased to work with BD Landscape Architects on the design of the Living Wetland Theatre and Aviary at WWT Slimbridge, which opened in 2021. Working with an emerging practice meant that we received a really personal service and Rob and his team were always ready to discuss and refine the project round the table. As a client we know we can be demanding, but I was pleased to welcome the whole practice to view the work on the ground and see their willingness to learn from the experience and develop their team's skills.

Simon Rose (Head of Experience Development, WWT)

Living Wetland Theatre

Exit

Waterscapes Aviary and Living Wetland Theatre

by Simon Rose (Head of Experience Developments, WWT)

A Conservation Legacy

WWT Slimbridge was established by Sir Peter Scott in 1946, becoming the first of ten sites currently operated by WWT, the charity for wetlands and wildlife. Situated on the banks of the River Severn in Gloucestershire and bordered by the Gloucester & Sharpness Canal, Slimbridge occupies a unique position on what is essentially an island of low-lying land—an ideal setting for a wetland conservation centre.

Scott's vision was revolutionary for its time. When he opened the doors of his wildfowl collection and research facility to the public, he was introducing a novel concept: nature conservation through public engagement. His philosophy was simple yet profound—to save nature, people must first learn to love it. This approach provided both an educational resource and a recreational destination for people enjoying increased leisure time and mobility in post-war Britain.

Over the decades, Slimbridge has transformed from what could be described as a 'stamp collection' of wildfowl into an immersive visitor experience, featuring live interpretation, hands-on activities, and presentations. The Living Wetland Theatre and Waterscapes Aviary was the flagship project for Slimbridge 2020, a co-ordinated package of works funded by the National Lottery Heritage Fund.

This ambitious initiative aimed to honour Scott's legacy while reimagining Slimbridge as a visitor centre equipped for the environmental challenges and educational opportunities of the 21st century.

Collaborative Design

The journey from concept to completion for the project began with a series of consultation meetings between the WWT team at Slimbridge and Kay Elliott Architects. These collaborative sessions were crucial in developing a vision for an interactive presentation space connected to an exhibit showcasing UK wetland habitats. In 2016, BD Landscape Architects joined the project to develop the landscape concept through to a technical design. Despite construction challenges posed by the global pandemic, the project reached completion in late 2020, with the official opening ceremony taking place in September 2021. This timing was significant, as it coincided with the 75th anniversary of the founding of Slimbridge.

Sustainability at Heart

Wetlands are recognized as the most effective carbon sinks on the planet, and the aviary offers visitors a microcosm of the range of wetland habitats found in the UK, ranging from wet woodland to freshwater streams, ponds, reedbeds, and an estuarine lagoon. However the development required some difficult decisions, including the demolition of the Tropical House, a 1960s structure of single-skin blockwork and polycarbonate roof. Despite being a well-loved exhibit, the building's lack of insulation, high internal temperature requirements provided by an old oil-fired boiler made it both energy-intensive and costly to operate. A commitment to sustainability as an integral part of Slimbridge operations made the decision to demolish more palatable, unlocking the site's potential for development. Environmental responsibility extended to the construction process itself, with the crushed concrete from the former tropical house incorporated into the amphitheatre seating. Other site-won materials, such as Forest of Dean Pennant stone boulders, were repurposed in the stream channel within the aviary. Existing willow pollards were carefully removed and replanted elsewhere on the site, where the high ground water table encourages easy establishment. The project team sourced reclaimed sea groynes on which to mount the theatre presentation screen and interpretation boards within the aviary and forming a 'break water' disguising the pump controlling water levels in the lagoon. An old wooden boat with bowsprit salvaged from a Devon boatyard added further character and appropriate perching for birds within the aviary.

Innovative Water Management

The water management system serves as both a practical solution and an educational tool. Rainwater fed tanks in the theatre seating area provide a demonstrable Sustainable Drainage System (SuDS), allowing visitors to visualize how rainwater is captured from the canopy, fed into the theatre pond, and back to the watercourse. The main water supply for the exhibit comes from the Gloucester and Sharpness Canal, which itself draws water from the River Severn in Gloucester. This water supplies the majority of the wetlands within the Centre before being returned to the river via a large reedbed wetland treatment system. This closed-loop approach extends to waste management as well: water from the toilet block is pumped to join wastewater from the main visitor centre, then directed to a purpose-built multi-stage reedbed for initial treatment before passing through the main reedbed and ultimately returning to the river.

Climate Resilience and Conservation

WWT's mission is clear and urgent: to restore wetlands, unlock their power, and empower others to do the same. The Waterscapes Aviary and Living Wetland Theatre are perfectly positioned to advance this mission by telling compelling stories about UK wetlands and how they are responding to climate change.

The exhibit showcases some species which were considered rare when Slimbridge was founded, such as avocets and egrets, but which are increasingly common in British wetlands today. These species serve as indicators for climate change, their pattern of distribution moving ever further northwards providing tangible evidence of shifting ecological conditions. The theatre presentations allow visitors to understand the dynamic nature of wetland ecosystems and the importance of conservation efforts in the face of global environmental challenges.

The relevance of WWT's work today cannot be overstated. Globally, wetlands are disappearing at an alarming rate - approximately 35% of the world's wetlands have been lost since 1970, a rate three times faster than forest loss. In the UK alone it is estimated that 75% of our wetlands have been drained for agriculture, or lost to development since 1700, most of this in the last century. These statistics represent not just a staggering loss of habitat, but a diminishing of all the other services wetland ecosystems provide, from water purification, flood protection and carbon sequestration to the positive feelings we derive from being close to water.

The Visitor Experience

The Living Wetland Theatre and Waterscapes Aviary form a significant part of the visitor experience within the grounds at Slimbridge and serve as a valuable resource for interactive learning, research, and conservation. The design prioritizes both the needs of the avian inhabitants and the human visitors, creating a space where authentic wildlife encounters can occur.

While the aviary primarily serves as a home for its bird species, its design prioritizes full accessibility, allowing people of all ages and abilities to get close to nature. The facility's commitment to accessibility ensures that able-bodied visitors, those with mobility challenges, wheelchair users, and families with young children in pushchairs can all share in the experience.

The design recognizes that meaningful conservation engagement requires breaking down barriers between people and nature. By creating spaces where visitors can observe wildlife up close in naturalistic settings, the facility fosters the emotional connections that encourage commitment to conservation.

Nature Up Close

The Aviary is designed to provide appropriate habitats for the wetland bird species it houses, allowing the birds to feel secure enough to exhibit natural behaviour, including nest-building and breeding. Visitors are treated to remarkable sights: waders running around, almost underfoot, and egrets perching gracefully in the trees. These close encounters create memorable experiences that foster a deeper connection with and appreciation for wetland wildlife.

The Theatre provides opportunities for interactive presentations and free flight demonstrations that appeal to visitors of all ages. These presentations are an opportunity to disseminate information and educational content to diverse audiences. Whether it' families sharing experiences that will be remembered for years to come, school groups returning home excited to tell family and friends about their adventures, or individuals inspired by the outdoor environment to pursue related hobbies or even careers, the impact of these experiences can extend far beyond the visit itself. The facility has been formally recognized - in 2021 Slimbridge was awarded an impressive 96% rating in the Visit England Quality Assured Visitor Attraction Assessment, an accolade that speaks to the effectiveness of the site's approach to public engagement and education.

A Model for Future Conservation Centres

As climate change and habitat loss continue to threaten wetland ecosystems worldwide, visitor centres like Slimbridge will play an increasingly vital role in raising awareness and inspiring action. The Waterscapes Aviary and Living Wetland Theatre exemplify how thoughtful design and innovative approaches can transform conservation education from passive observation to active engagement.

As we face increasing environmental challenges, the work being done at Slimbridge reminds us that effective conservation requires both scientific understanding and public engagement. By continuing to evolve and adapt, WWT Slimbridge ensures that Sir Peter Scott's legacy will endure, inspiring visitors to love and protect wetlands for generations to come.

"As much as we need air to breathe, we need water to live. The conservation of our wetlands is essential to life on Earth."

Simon has over forty years' experience in the landscape industry. Starting off on a commercial nursery he cut his conservation teeth with the Urban Wildlife Group in Birmingham, before spending a few valuable years in local authority. Simon is now Head of Experience Developments at WWT, where he leads a team designing and building exhibits and other projects at wetland centres in the UK.

Work includes gardens, pond zones, canoe safaris and 'wild walks', animal and bird exhibits, conservation breeding projects and hides, as well as less glamourous but essential infrastructure work. Much of his work has focused on promoting the benefits of wetlands, from the smallest rain gardens at the end of a down-pipe, to Steart Marshes, a 500ha flood alleviation project on the Bristol Channel, now managed as a wetland nature reserve by WWT.

6

Learning Outside the Classroom

Mulberry Academy – London Dock

The new Mulberry Academy sits within the London Dock by St George development, delivering hundreds of new homes and school places to the thriving London Borough of Tower Hamlets.

Within the wider Mulberry Academy – London Dock masterplan, the site was allocated for a six-form entry secondary school, as well as a 250-place sixth form centre. This provides much needed spaces for local children and young people, with an expected student number of 1,200 on a tight 0.5 hectare site.

Our vision was to deliver a cherished community asset which provides essential educational resources alongside community activities. Our designs draw on the site's rich history and context – it lies between the local square of Merino Gardens and the A1203, on the site of vast former warehouses – to celebrate the character of the local area. Alongside its hyper-urban character, we also wanted to express native landscapes of shady woodland, marginal grasslands, and river edges which would once have inhabited this riverine area.

Our landscape proposals therefore seek to create natural systems to help mitigate the negative impacts to the school from its surrounding urban fabric – such as noise and pollution – as well as an environment supportive of local ecology, play, learning and work.

For such a compact site, our designs needed to focus on a multi-layered landscape with playgrounds, social and teaching spaces over numerous ground floor, podium, and roof levels. The multifaceted green infrastructure of new tree planting, green walls, lushly-filled raised planters and biodiverse roofs contributes massively to the area's urban greening. It connects the site into its local biodiversity, as well as creating a calm, green environment for learners. A plethora of seating opportunities and open spaces provides for every young person, with the green setting encouraging a connection to plants and the outdoors.

BD's involvement ran from concept to completion over eight busy years, where we enjoyed working closely with fellow disciplines to provide a really hard-working, three-dimensional landscape.

London Dock Secondary School

"I like how it's very spacious, having a spacious environment gives you a spacious mind."

Year 7 Student

Ivydale Primary School

"We are really happy, we've seen an immediate improvement in behaviour around school - it's absolutely proved to us that, actually, the school environment makes a huge difference to how children learn..."

Helen Ingham (Headteacher)

The expansion of Ivydale School presented a great opportunity to create valuable external play spaces beside the new buildings, embracing light and space to promote nature and emotional wellbeing for both pupils and teachers. Located in the diverse London Borough of Southwark, the school needed to double its capacity with the new site, as well as provide a more 'grown-up' space for the Key Stage 2 cohort.

Our sketch designs focused on a multi-use amphitheatre at the heart of the school's outdoor activities, which would also extend Ivydale's passion for performance and community. It would also make use of the existing stepped site, and provide a platform to blend between the different characters from our original vision: the open, sunny, social courtyard where people can gather and run; and the soft informal areas beyond.

The existing trees onsite provided us with a mature tree network to tie into. It also inspired the creation of a wild woodland garden specifically for use by forest schools, to set children on a life-long appreciation of nature. This valuable pocket of habitat includes an education corner, nature trail, and opportunities for willow craft.

Each ground floor classroom has its own outdoor extension where classes can spill out into. These include raised growing gardens to promote the importance of educational landscapes and local food production, and give each learner the opportunity to grow their own plants to use in lessons. An outdoor dining space with permanent colourful canopies also provides shelter, shade and a social seating area.

Since the school's completion, it has won a 2018 RIBA London Award, with the Judges noting the successes of the integrated design with the Hawkins\Brown building, the varied play, and the opportunities for outdoor learning.

Soft Informal
Playspace & Structured Play
Existing Tree
with Deck
Hard Social
Playspace
MUGA
Play Mound
Play element with new tree planting
using spoil from site
Amphitheatre steps
To create a performance
area on the lower
terrace and
accommodate the change
in level across site
Growing Gardens
Raised planters provide
students with
access to their own
productive landscape

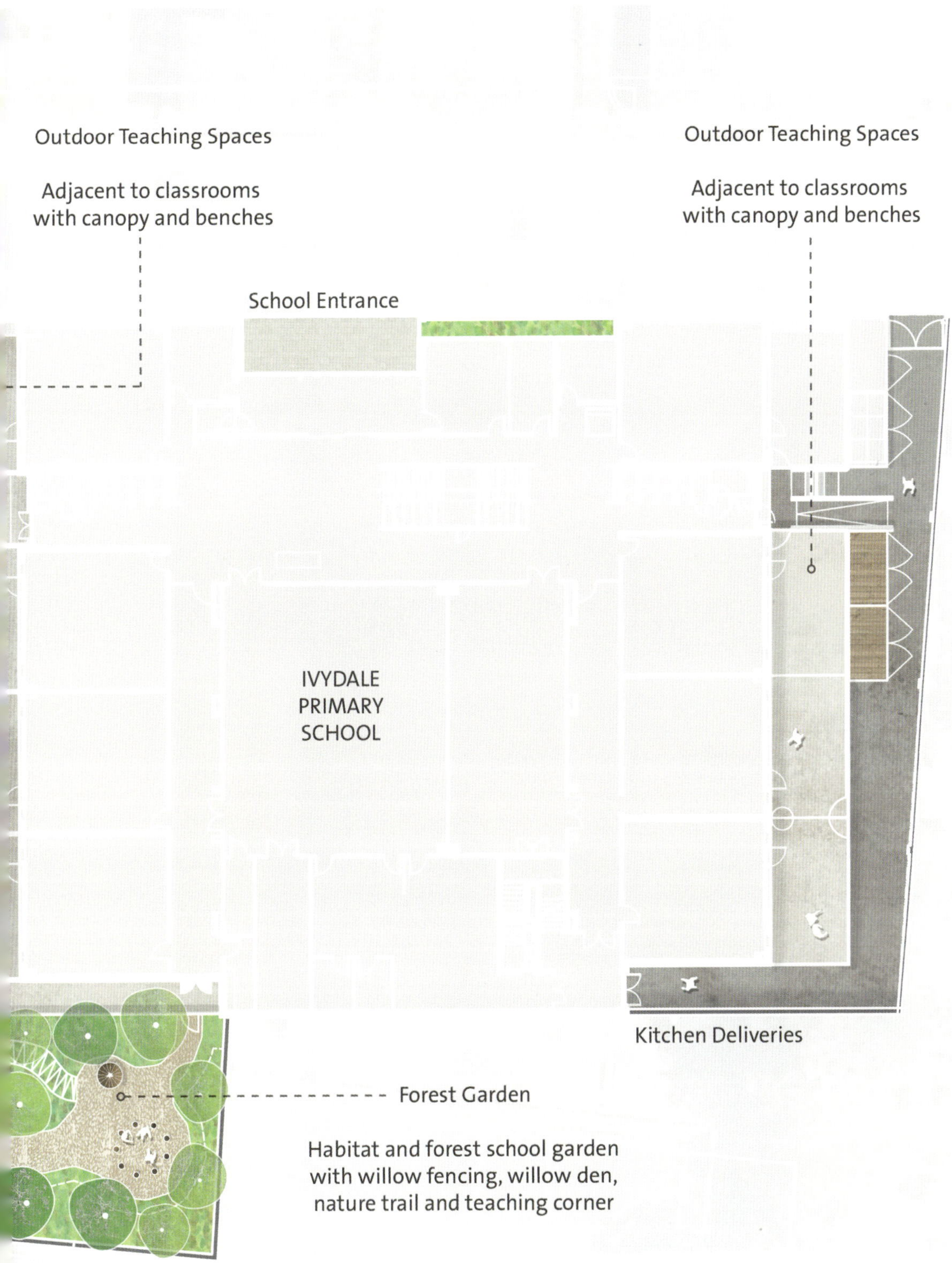
Outdoor Teaching Spaces
Adjacent to classrooms with canopy and benches
School Entrance
Outdoor Teaching Spaces
Adjacent to classrooms with canopy and benches
IVYDALE PRIMARY SCHOOL
Kitchen Deliveries
Forest Garden
Habitat and forest school garden with willow fencing, willow den, nature trail and teaching corner

Planting
Soft informal play area
Amphitheatre steps
Hard play
Flexible Lower Terrace
External Classroom

GDST Notting Hill + Ealing School

The Girls' Day School Trust appointed BD alongside long-term collaborators Hawkins\Brown to develop a concept which would transform their tired and inaccessible junior school grounds. This constrained site is set within the beautiful, leafy historic suburbs of Ealing, with the wider campus being home to the school since 1930.

The designs provide a high-quality teaching environment both internally and externally. The architecture provides new classrooms and specialist spaces for a library, arts, music and IT, alongside an integrated landscape which has resolved the previous accessibility issues around the site.

As pupils and parents approach the school, they will note its hugely improved street presence. The school is friendly and visible, with a clear entrance and welcome for pupils, carers and visitors. This sets the school as a key local building, enhancing its local area through sensitive incorporation of existing trees and hedgerows, plus options for stepped and flush entrances into the building.

We really enjoyed the careful development of the designs alongside the school. One of the main aims of the landscape design was to create coherent and accessible routes throughout a site with very complex levels, so that pupils could easily navigate it. We also wanted to maximise opportunities for learning outside the classroom.

We designed a series of high-quality external spaces to support the built form. These include a planted welcome garden, forest school and outdoor teaching space, plus a separate and secure reception year play space. Each area carefully considered the combination of play and learning to give that holistic, hard-working landscape the school required. A plethora of new trees – including maples, birches, and small-leaved limes – provide an intimate, sheltered landscape with all the benefits of shade, bird and insect life, plus autumn colour.

"With a science garden, forest school area, dedicated play area for Reception pupils and an additional playground for other year groups, the outside space is beautifully landscaped with lots of trees and is integral to making learning a hands-on experience."

Emma Santamaria (Senior Associate, BD)

GDST Notting Hill + Ealing School

Tiger Way Primary School

Nightingale School is part of the wider 'Tiger Way' project which we have designed from concept in 2014 to completion in 2019. The scheme delivers a new primary school and nursery, providing much needed school spaces for the London Borough of Hackney, funded through the sale of 89 high-quality residential apartments co-located on the same site (The Otto), and delivered with McLaren Construction.

At 4,900 square metres, the landscape challenge was to create excellent school grounds for learning outside the classroom, on a very constrained, dense site. As the built form developed, we were asked to sketch out a total of six outdoor spaces for the school. These would be spread across a series of ground level and raised terraces, and gave us an opportunity to create an innovative and high-quality learning environment. Care was taken to balance the needs of the different stakeholders, residents and pupils to produce co-existing landscapes for both Nightingale and The Otto, which did not detract from each other.

Our concept focused on the fantastical picture book 'Where the Wild Things Are' to unite play spaces for nursery, reception and Key Stage 1 years. This is a magical place where imaginations can run wild – and we wanted to encourage adventure, role play, and a variety of different play experiences within the landscape. Play time should be an opportunity for the pupils to 'run wild' before heading back into school for formal learning.

We wanted to encourage a mix of natural and prescribed play through clever use of equipment. This has translated to a range of related elements – from stone boulders to climbing structures, swings to slides, and running tracks to secret dens – giving variation and balance to the spaces. This mix aids development of key motor and physical skills, as well as

"We've noticed how our youngest children have gained great spatial awareness and climbing skills through their interactions with the environment in the EYFS playground. It's great to see them clambering on the rocks and playing together in the stream."

Abigail Hopper (Nightingale Headteacher)

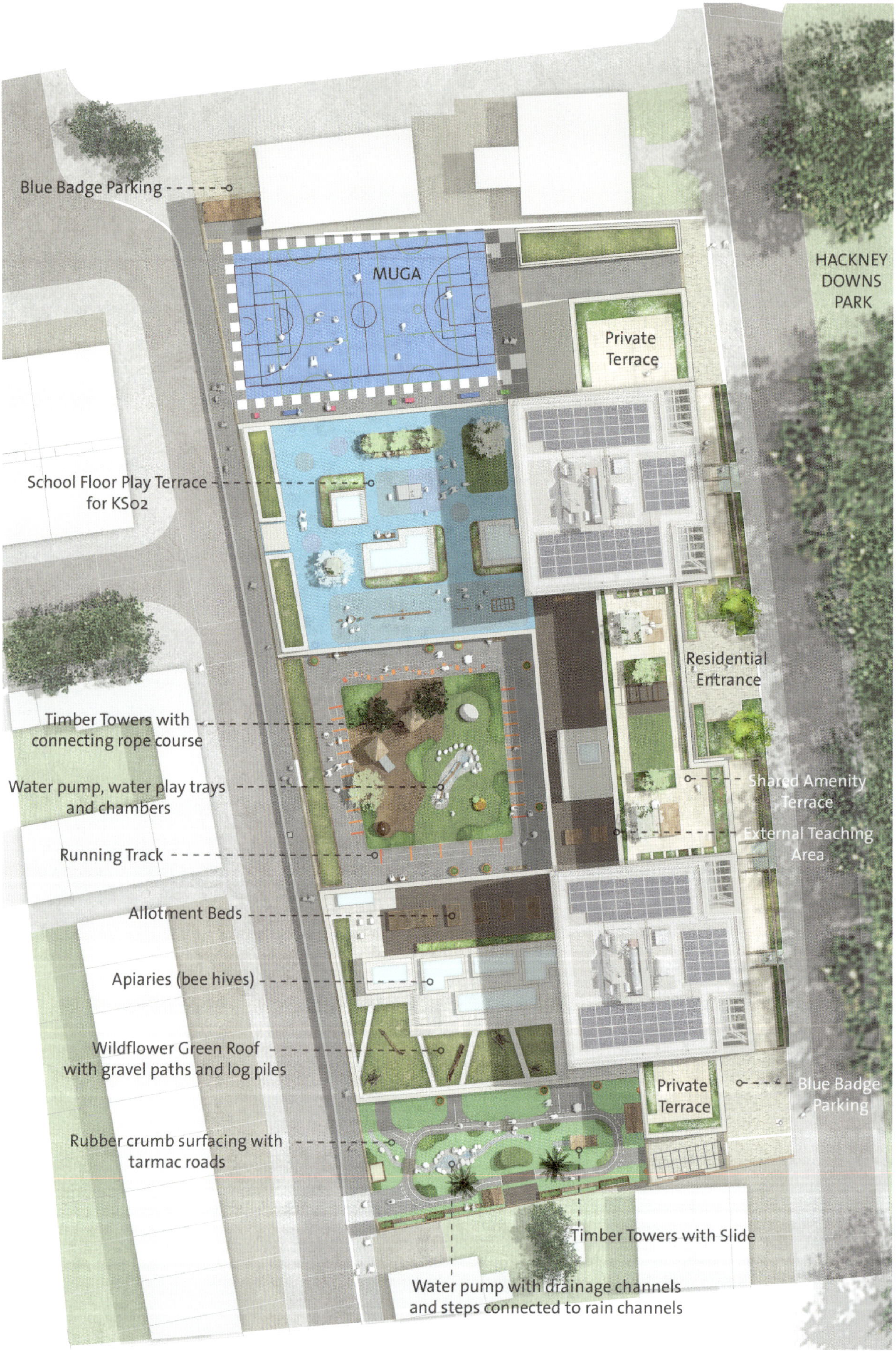
Blue Badge Parking
MUGA
HACKNEY DOWNS PARK
Private Terrace
School Floor Play Terrace for KSO2
Residential Entrance
Timber Towers with connecting rope course
Water pump, water play trays and chambers
Shared Amenity Terrace
External Teaching Area
Running Track
Allotment Beds
Apiaries (bee hives)
Wildflower Green Roof with gravel paths and log piles
Private Terrace
Blue Badge Parking
Rubber crumb surfacing with tarmac roads
Timber Towers with Slide
Water pump with drainage channels and steps connected to rain channels

encouraging the imaginative role play from our vision. We always encourage the use of water play, and use it to great effect at Nightingale to tie into the concept of Max's journey across the water in 'Where the Wild Things Are'. The central feature of a water pump can be used by multiple pupils, and they can explore how water levels change downstream through play and involvement from others.

One of the project's challenges was to ensure that Nightingale, within the wider Tiger Way scheme, felt like a coherent whole. The landscape's material palette therefore ties in carefully to that of the architectural façade: a seamless transition between the vertical and horizontal elements creating a coherent and visually restful scheme. The site sits opposite the leafy Hackney Downs Park, bordered with mature London plane trees; as such the textured material approach aims to blend the built form into its park setting. Careful design of circulation and entrances has also combined the school and residential uses seamlessly on one site, without compromising the quality, functionality or operation of the outdoor spaces.

The school's upper level play decks include a wide variety of spaces for learning outside the classroom. Wildflower living roofs give children the opportunity to get close to wild plants, with a complementary bee keeping area offering further practical knowledge of biodiversity and pollination. Areas for active play, a Multi Use Games Area, and productive 'grow your own' beds provide further adventurous play and learning experiences.

We also enjoyed working with other disciplines to turn elements that often detract from the landscape, such as rain water pipes, into playful elements of the scheme. This team collaboration has helped to produce a truly innovative and playful landscape throughout.

The wider Tiger Way scheme achieved BREEAM Outstanding at design stage, and in 2018 won a BREEAM Award for the best public project at design stage. From our first involvement at concept stage, through to the project's completion with McClaren Construction, Nightingale School developed and progressed with the involvement of all stakeholders to ensure there were no compromises made later on. Every external space has a purpose and has been used to maximise the play, biodiversity and amenity value to each user.

For us, the success of a good school landscape can be measured in the enjoyment, engagement and interaction of the children who use it:

"The children are engaged, enthusiastic and always excited in their playgrounds, they are absolutely loving them. We're all very grateful for BD's expertise and all proud of the outcome."

Nicolas Laurent,
(Authority's Client and Technical Adviser)

"BD landscape architects excelled in the challenge we set them to create engaging and educational playgrounds on a tight site to cover the whole Primary curriculum at Nightingale Primary School. In response to the Headteacher's demanding need for creative solutions, they produced beautiful fun spaces, full of nature and ecology, that provide teachers a wide range of learning opportunities strongly linked with their curriculum needs."

Nicolas Laurent (Authority's Client and Technical Adviser)

Tiger Way Primary School

Emmanuel Primary School

"BD landscape architects enabled plans for a learning and educational landscape that incorporates flexible external spaces, makes use of the level change through the site for games & learning and has external learning decks linked to the teaching areas. Extensive consultation with the students and staff gave the project team a clear direction to develop the external spaces."

Tracy Kilkenny (Head of School, Emmanuel CE Primary School)

Emmanuel Church of England Primary School lies in the heart of West Hampstead, in the vibrant London Borough of Camden. They serve the whole community and have always aimed to provide their pupils with a happy and stimulating place to learn – values we wanted to embody in their landscape.

In collaboration with Hawkins\Brown architects, Max Fordham and Elliot Wood engineers, BD worked on the redevelopment of Emmanuel's existing site to provide an Early Years Foundation Unit, alongside this brand new one-form entry primary school. This was funded as a joint project between Camden and the London Diocesan Board for Schools.

We loved engaging with the existing school community, and extensive consultation with students and staff gave us a clear direction to develop the external spaces.

Our designs focused on the landscape as a part of the learning and educational environment, with flexible external spaces that would cater for multiple groups from individual classes to outdoor assemblies, and everything in between. Our proposals also make use of the existing level change, with terraces dividing the grounds into different play uses – perfect for games and learning. The finished landscape has subtle learning weaved throughout.

The colourful terrace at the heart of the school teaches children the rainbow colours and acts as an exciting focal point for gathering. Outdoor classrooms, productive 'edible' gardens, green walls and a Multi-Use Games Area were also incorporated within our designs.

The design has also enhanced the ecological value of the site, with new habitats – including native climbing plants, trees, hedges and species-rich edible garden – tailored to the local biodiversity action plan.

The Value of Learning Outside the Classroom

by Carol Lees (Hawkins\Brown)

What I love about working on school projects is that we are able to create environments which inspire, stimulate and nurture children and young people through their most formative years.

In recent years, we've seen a broader evolution in education aimed at making schools more flexible, inclusive, and responsive to the needs of modern society. Schools have a responsibility to ensure our children grow, not only academically but also physically, socially, and emotionally and a fantastic school environment supports them to do this.

The requirements of the inside of a school haven't changed much over the last decade. As architects, we know the components of a successful classroom – well proportioned, appropriate storage, lots of display, flooded with natural light, good acoustics, no glare, air quality, comfortable temperature etc. Generally children start with a consistent formal classroom base in the younger years, which becomes more flexible as they grow older and they transition through secondary school.

However, a school's external spaces can be considered the 'laboratory of education'. Creating diverse and accessible outdoor areas ensures that all students can participate and benefit from being outside. Landscaped areas encourage physical activity, essential for students' physical and mental well-being. Outdoor classrooms enhance learning experiences, enabling pupils to engage with nature and the environment. Well considered outdoor areas in schools ensure our children have access to the ultimate free flow, self-directed play and learning spaces, and perhaps more importantly, the defining place where our young people learn how to interact and socialise with others.

At Hawkins\Brown, we're always looking at how we can improve health and support wellbeing. We know that the UK is facing a significant obesity crisis, with high rates of both adult and childhood obesity. Modern life makes fewer physical demands on many people, who lead less active lifestyles as technology replaces the need for physical activity. Statistics published by the Department for Transport show that children have been walking and cycling to school less and less, with increasing reliance on cars - 67% in 1975-76 to just 47% in 2023. They also reported that in London the school run contributes to one in four cars on urban roads at peak times, even in such a densely populated area.

We are committed to designing for health across all our projects and this is particularly important in schools. We need to support our young people and their health. Being in nature benefits wellbeing beyond just exercise. Instilling a love of nature at an early age encourages them to care for their environment and not repeat the mistakes of previous generations.

Collaborating with BD Landscape has always been easy because we care about the same things. User experience is front and centre in our projects, and this is the thread that connects us. Together, we have worked on multiple school projects over the last decade and beyond. We are equally ambitious for our projects. We want them to be impactful for the school communities and be the best they can be.

This ambition was particularly evident at Cherry Garden SEN School where all classrooms wrapped around ground floor play spaces, ensuring direct access to nature and the seasons throughout the year. Being inclusive did not mean dumbing down – on the contrary the landscape scheme provided interest, stimulation and choice for its pupils through provision of elevated walkways, sensory planting and natural play spaces.

Similarly, who would have thought you could have beehives in a school playground on a roof terrace in central London? This is what we did at Tiger Way in Hackney. We developed a two storey primary school with residential apartments directly above. The shape of the building and playspaces were very much determined by rights of light, and ensuring the taller housing did not impact the external playspace. Rooftop terraces for residents peer out over the park but within sight of dedicated rooftop spaces for the children, including play spaces on one and a wildflower garden and beekeeping space on the other. It was ambitious and rather fabulous.

When I think back to conversations with BD at the outset of projects, they were always to discuss people and users. I remember an early engagement session with the pupils of Emmanuel C of E Primary school in Camden. As we stood on the new site, Rob scattered a mountain of laminated images – showing a variety of landscapes, play equipment and planting – and asked pupils to select one, hold it above their head and explain what they liked. Lots of laughter and enthusiasm ensued. That's how to talk about design and schools with children.

Carol is a Partner at Hawkins\Brown and has over 20 years of experience working in the education sector. Her portfolio extends from nurseries and schools through to higher education and science research institutes. Projects include schools for the Girls Day School Trust and the City of London, and the Laboratory of Medical Sciences for the MRC / Imperial College. Carol is passionate about the impact good design can have in an educational environment.

She championed Hawkins\Brown's #GreatSchools initiative in partnership with the Architects Journal, is a member of the school group on the Essex Quality Review Panel and has participated as an expert panel member in debates about school design today. She is also a chair of governors at a local primary school in Hackney.

7 Community

Family Welcome Centre

Harold Hill's innovative Family Welcome Centre is expected to be the first of its kind - providing short-term accommodation for vulnerable families whilst permanent housing is found for them. The project will form a key part of the wider Farnham and Hilldene Estate regeneration including a revitalised local district centre.

We were appointed by the London Borough of Havering at the initial design stages, and have enjoyed once again working alongside Hawkins\Brown. Their initial architectural sketches showed how important the landscape would be at the Welcome Centre – the high-density building wrapping around a central heart of courtyard. This will provide future residents with vital outdoor space to socialise, relax, and connect with nature.

Our designs welcome residents from the public realm: new street tree planting lead you towards the Centre, and frames views alongside richly planted rain gardens. These also invite nature in for the local community, and capture rainwater run-off from the wide entrance pavement as part of the sustainable drainage strategy.

For the courtyard, our aspiration was to provide an appealing collage of spaces to cater for the broad mix of different backgrounds and ages likely to call this place home.

We saw natural play as a great opportunity for a range of children and young people to play, as well as a beautiful setting for residents to look onto. It has therefore been woven throughout the courtyard, with salvaged timber, playful mounds, textures of sand and grass, and stepping stones. Carefully incorporated swing, slide and musical chimes also provide a range of equipped play for varied abilities and ages. There is also playful surfacing with space to stretch and scoot.

Secluded seating pockets amongst new trees and biodiverse planting will provide opportunity for reflection and relaxation, and an edible corner with fruit trees encourages community harvests.

The Centre received planning in 2022 and is swiftly progressing through construction – we can't wait to see it open its doors to families in the near future.

"It's been fantastic to be a part of this pioneering project – working closely with Havering and such a talented design team to deliver resilient, hard-working, hopeful spaces for future residents."

Cat Thomas (Associate Landscape Architect, BD)

Wallbridge

Wallbridge forms the southern gateway to the market town of Stroud. With the canal running through the site and the presence of old brewery walls, it has significant cultural and historical importance for the town. Today however, Wallbridge is a neglected and under-used space, dominated by the air and noise pollution of encircling cars.

Stroud District Council highlighted Wallbridge within their planned applications to the Levelling Up Fund, and in 2022 appointed BD to develop the public realm.

With Wallbridge, we saw a great potential to engage directly with the public to inform our collaborative approach to the masterplan. Our initial stakeholder engagement took place during March and April 2022 with Stroud District Council, Gloucestershire County Council and other local groups. Engagement with the Stroud Local History Society also helped us to understand Wallbridge's development from thriving commerce centre to a place of movement and arrival.

From this, our concept masterplan developed: to transform the area into a vibrant, attractive green space.

We really enjoyed taking this concept – along with artistic visuals and a scale model – to the public in the May: talking through our designs and taking comments and questions from over 200 visitors. Through these sessions and an online platform we gained valuable positive feedback and local insight: a desire to reduce vehicle impact; improve access on foot and bike; create wildlife links; and incorporate local art informed by Stroud's art scene.

Our final design united this engagement into the design you can see – a hardworking space for Stroud. A widened towpath and viewing platform reference the historic landscape and connects people meaningfully to the canal. Wildflower meadows and impressive tree planting buffers traffic and connects to existing green and blue infrastructure. High-quality flexible spaces also improve circulation, with plenty of opportunities for pop-up events and gatherings to extend Stroud's sense of pride in their town.

1
TRAIN STATION

2

3

Filwood Community Centre

This much-loved community centre lies in the heart of Knowle West in south Bristol. We were delighted to be part of the winning competition team for Bristol City Council's major retrofit of the Centre – the flagship for wider regeneration of Filwood Broadway – and began work on the Centre's early design stages in 2023.

The redesign of the Community Centre includes a completely refreshed façade to the 1938 building, relocated public library, and brand-new public living room, all by Hayhurst and Co architects and Integral Engineering Design. We have really enjoyed sketching out our landscape designs alongside their reworking of the building – focusing on refreshed public realm to the two key street corners, and a centrepiece of two inner community courtyards.

The designs, including those for the landscape, have been developed using a wealth of input from local people after an extensive community engagement process, aiming to put the people of Filwood at their heart. To engage with as wide a variety of people as possible, You&Me architecture led on a programme that included: shop window displays using scale model maquettes; local history walks; drop-in sessions; Filwood Fair stalls; and school assemblies. These all gathered people's ideas and views to input into our developing designs. A particular highlight was the 'Filwood is Growing' pilot project on the key corner of Barnstaple Road – where we input to designs for colourful raised beds to extend the community growing already taking place on site.

As part of the project, we have also been involved with Knowle West Media Centre's (KWMC) work experience programme. This partnered with the wider design team to introduce local young people to the fields of landscape architecture, engineering, architecture, and more. Across two weeks, we had a fantastic time taking groups through a fun and challenging design exercise using their Community Centre as the real-world application. We developed with them a landscape design brief based on their interests, and guided them through concept themes and design sketches as they dreamt ideas for Filwood's central courtyard. We loved watching their ideas come to life through making sessions at KWMC's 'The Factory', which included 3D modelling, printing and crafting of physical prototypes; followed by a celebration of each design as part of group crits.

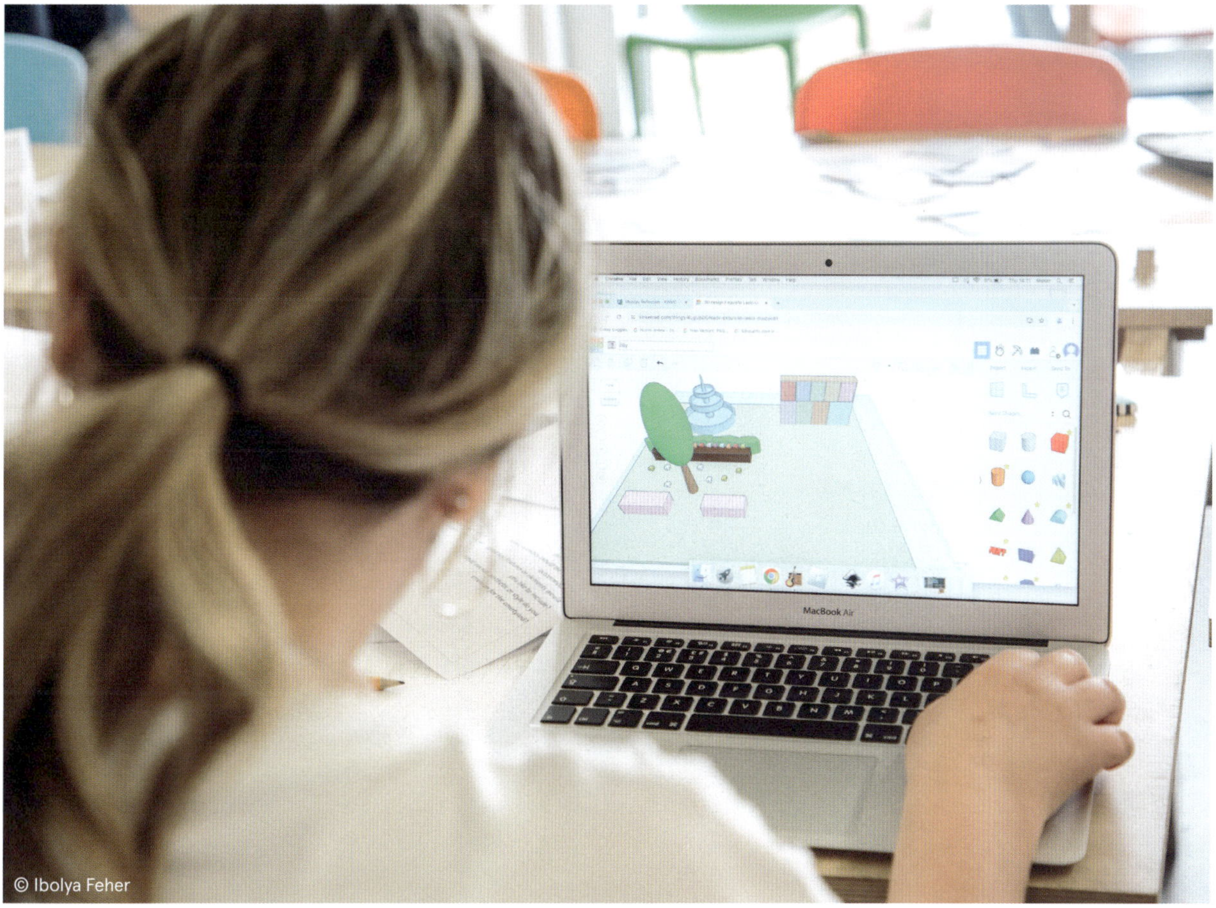
MacBook Air
© Ibolya Feher

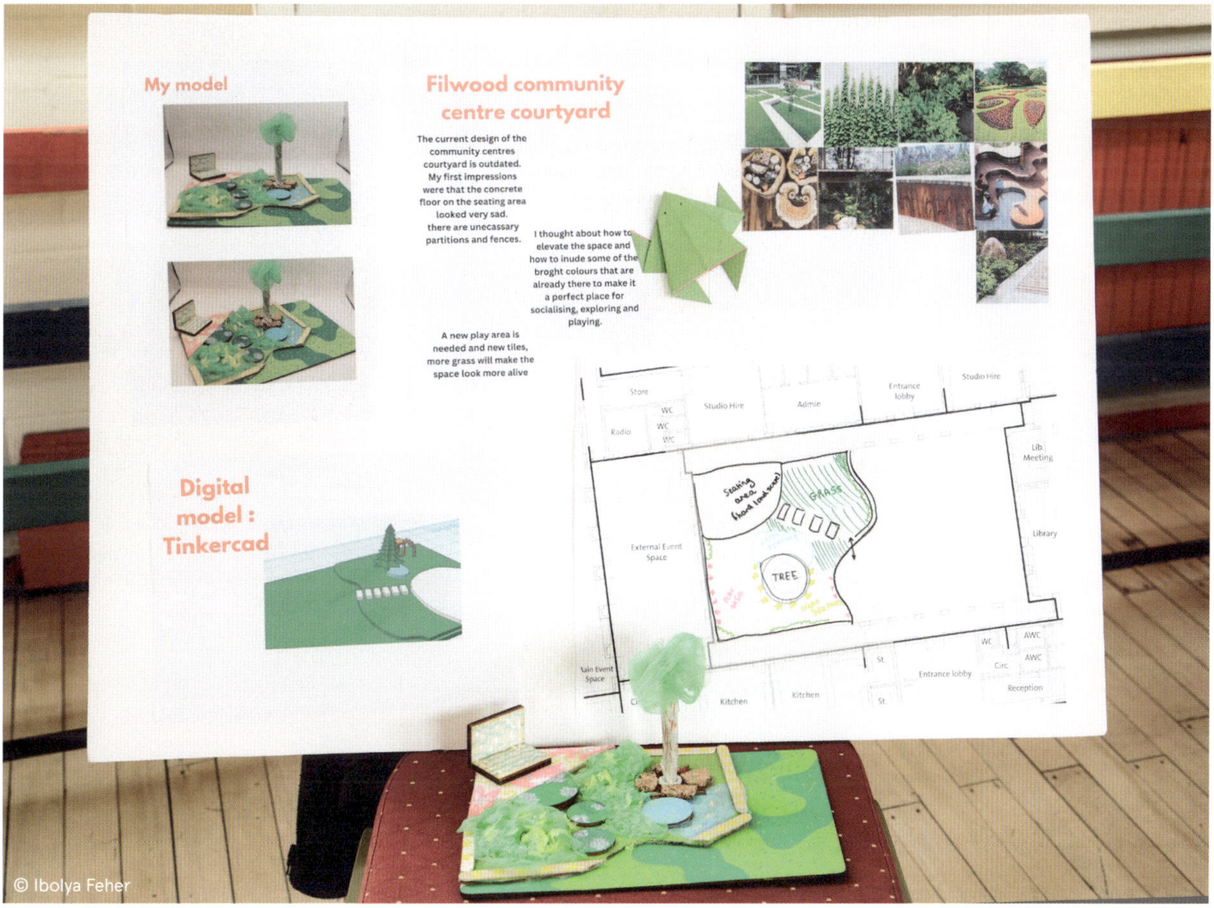
My model
Filwood community centre courtyard
The current design of the community centres courtyard is outdated. My first impressions were that the concrete floor on the seating area looked very sad. there are unecassary partitions and fences.
I thought about how to elevate the space and how to inude some of the broght colours that are already there to make it a perfect place for socialising, exploring and playing.
A new play area is needed and new tiles, more grass will make the space look more alive
Digital model : Tinkercad
Store
Radio
WC
WC
WC
Studio Hire
Admin
Entrance lobby
Studio Hire
Lib. Meeting
Library
External Event Space
TREE
GRASS
Kitchen
Kitchen
St.
St.
Entrance lobby
Circ.
WC
AWC
AWC
Reception
© Ibolya Feher

New Tree Planting to public realm
Events vehicle parking
Programmatic space with event seating
Flexible space for group activities
Allotment and growing space
Playful sunken zone around existing tree
Enhanced biodiversity
Native hedgerow and tree planting
Richly planted raingardens
The 'Gem' courtyard an intimate learning space with lush raingarden planting
Partly-sunken spill-out space to the studio
Workshop parking
Enhanced biodiversity with natural seating

We were inspired by the young people's desire to weave wildlife and water through their plans, as well as their use of bold colours and patterns. We aim to embody this additional layer of local engagement through the final finessing of our designs during construction.

Our designs focus on the two courtyard spaces being redrawn at the heart of the Community Centre. We loved the public feedback that these should be 'oases', and have therefore imagined them as richly planted spaces, integrated completely within the sustainable drainage strategy as large-scale rain gardens. It was important for the largest courtyard to feature flexible space for events to spill-out from the newly refurbished main hall; the smaller courtyard also needed to tie into the neighbouring adult and children's library spaces, providing outdoor reading groups and secluded pockets. The levels design had to carefully respond to the variety of existing building thresholds and several retained structural features, all whilst providing accessible circulation for all.

A key aspiration for us was to celebrate the re-use of the Community Centre's landscape elements and materials wherever possible. These include two courtyard memorial trees which we have sensitively incorporated, and which will act as an anchor of familiar presence amongst the wider changes. Demolition materials such as brick from the Centre's defunct skittle alley will be used within courtyard gabions as habitat features; and the building's red brick walls picked out through UK-manufactured clay pavers across the landscape. Rainwater will also be captured from the Centre's rooftops and attenuated in a series of connected rain gardens. These will treat and slowly filter rainwater, as well as provide a lushly planted, biophilic setting of colourful perennials, shrubs and bulbs for the community and pollinators to enjoy.

A communal growing hub is another important feature of the landscape, and will continue the excellent food-growing culture on site through the work of local organisations such as the Square Food Foundation.

The building's new façade will be complemented by artistic metalwork, flowering meadows and tree planting, which will help to lift the external realm and invite the community in. A lively border of colourful perennials and new street trees will frame the Community Centre, and help to lift the wider street scene.

Guide Dogs for the Blind

In 2021 Guide Dogs for the Blind commissioned BD to re-imagine their existing regional centre at Redbridge. With keen dog devotees in-house, we were thrilled to design the landscape for this centre which already trains around 250 guide dogs a year.

The site is located in Woodford Green in outer East London, constrained by the local green belt designation as well as the historic setting of the Claybury conservation area bounding the site to the south and east. The steeply sloping topography also provided us with many design opportunities and challenges.

We loved learning all about the life of a training guide dog to inform our designs, and it quickly became clear this landscape would need to work ultra hard to fulfil the needs of every human and dog using it. As well as safe, accessible and joyful access for staff and visitors, our designs needed to incorporate enrichment and training opportunities for the dogs with their handlers, alongside a variety of circulatory walking routes to assess their progress. It was also crucial to allow safe vehicular access both for servicing of the building, alongside the dropping off and collection of the guide dogs.

Our completed design for Redbridge brings visitors and staff up to the main building along a re-designed access track with integrated raingarden. This is diversely planted with grasses, shrubs and flowering perennials to welcome the eye, as well as capture and treat water run-off sustainably. Swathes of native wildflowers across the site also provides habitat for local pollinators and insects.
New, semi-mature tree planting provides succession alongside the existing tree-lined boundary, with additional native buffer planting providing a mosaic of connected corridors for wildlife. At the building's entrance a sensory garden delights visitors with tactile grasses, colour and scented flowers, and leads directly to the west-facing café terrace.

It was also crucial our designs followed all best practice for accessibility, and we enjoyed ensuring movement across Redbridge allowed access for all – carefully considering accessible gradients, pavement widths, and the visual materiality throughout.

"It has been such a pleasure to work with Guide Dogs UK and the wider design team to help deliver this project that will help facilitate their life-changing work for so many people for years to come."

Helen Kirk (Senior Associate, BD)

Way out

Guide Dogs for the Blind

Guide Dogs
Regional Centre
South East

ONE WAY
Visitor Reception

"When we started this project, we knew that the green belt status of the redevelopment land was going to be a vital part of it, and we wanted to make sure we did it right. Having BD Landscape Architects carefully add to the landscape around the new centre has given us a space that is not only a perfect space to train our dogs, but can also be used by our staff and service users to relax, and is a haven for local wildlife."

Anna Hoskyns (Senior Manager – Workplace Projects)

Cardinal Codesign

A core part of chapter one's Cardinal Place was our deeply meaningful community engagement, co-design, consultation and feedback sessions. These were led by BD and facilitated by social enterprise 2-3 Degrees and Soundings.

The approach to engagement involved six stages to involve a variety of users and help shape our proposals: (1) office worker questionnaires; (2) 'The Trial Phase'; (3) youth co-design; (4) consulting key stakeholders; (5) the social media launch; (6) the public consultation event.

We were really impressed by the young people we met in the youth sessions, and their genuine interest in shaping their environment.

The feedback from initial engagement was taken on board and presented back to the youth group. This allowed them to dissect and review their original proposals with fresh thinking, plus the knowledge we had imparted on how different roles in a design team work.

Alongside this exciting local youth engagement, the team consulted with a number of stakeholders: Westminster City Council, Victoria Neighbourhood Forum, Victoria BID, office customers and retail brand partners. All have been in person meetings, with feedback continually incorporated into the Cardinal designs.

In June 2023 we conducted a wider public consultation targeted at local resident groups, organisations and businesses. An online and social media campaign was launched to promote and build anticipation, with the dedicated Cardinal Place website presenting Landsec's ambition for the space and engaging close to 800 people.

The public consultation event was a comprehensive day of walking tours, workshops and art competitions. Through genuine conversations about access, social activities, biodiversity, and aesthetics, we captured the views of over 350 local residents, office workers and visitors.

"[I am] very happy that my voice is heard and that I can take part in the changes that are going to be done in Cardinal [Place]. I was able to improve on my creative side and communication and teamwork skills."

Young Person from Engagement Session

Central Heart
Cardinal Place
VICTORIA
We want to hear your thoughts on making the central zone at Cardinal Place more lively and exciting. What kind of events and activities would you like to see here?
Live music
Screening of live sport
Outdoor cinema
Community events
Outdoor fitness classes
Other
?
Scan this QR code to access more information about the Cardinal Place project proposals!
Cardinal Place

The Importance of Public Realm in Creating a Sense of Place and Community

by Rich Sansom (Landsec)

The proliferation of working from home since the COVID-19 pandemic has meant many employees have adequate, if not more tailored, work set ups in their home than they do at the office. As a result, employers need to "earn the commute" and provision of amenity spaces has been a key factor in office leasing activity in recent years. CBRE's Europe Office Occupier Sentiment Survey 2024 [1] indicated that 52% of occupiers surveyed are looking to relocate offices, with the need to offer better amenities and services to employees being cited as a top-3 driver. 73% of surveyed firms said that outdoor amenities, terrace, green space were a key consideration when choosing a new space. Improved public realm can provide employees with a space they may not have at home, particularly those who live in central London. An area to meet others, to congregate and to be amongst nature.

Public realm improvement is being seen across London with British Land's transformation of Exchange Square, Related Argent's continued investment into King's Cross and Granary Square and Landsec's investment into Cardinal Place amongst others. Landlord-developers are looking to encourage new office or retail occupiers and/ or entice more visitors to their estates. The capital outlay on public realm improvement projects is proportionally small when compared to the value of the estates that they sit within or alongside. A small increase in rental value, a letting of a previously unlet retail or office unit, or more footfall to a retail tenant on a turnover-based rent can all lead to returns on investment for public realm improvements that help to justify what is commonly considered as discretionary spend.

In retail, the shopping experience continues to be of key importance to driving footfall and therefore spend in shops. In many high streets, the public areas are often owned by the local council or similar authority, which limits the ability for landlords to improve the public realm immediately outside their shops. In certain key areas, such as Regent Street and the Strand, local authorities have been able to collaborate with landlords for hugely successful improvements to public space, however these collaborations are not simple and therefore do not always come to fruition. At Cardinal Place, we had a unique opportunity to improve both the retail landscape for the shops at ground floor level but also to provide a space for the 840,000 square feet of office space that surrounds it, all within Landsec's ownership.

We believe that public realm is the city's connective tissue and where its occupants interact. Well planned and delivered urban realm helps to connect communities. Cardinal Place was not offering this opportunity and, although the terrace was popular in summer months, the ground floor area was lacking in interest and was a largely transient space.

Working with BD Landscape Architects, we were able to distil our vision for the space into 4 simple but key objectives:

1. Capture people's attention
2. Draw them in
3. Encourage them to stay
4. Get them to return

It was hugely important that the improvement works were designed and completed with the local community and the users of the space. After extensive research and surveying, we were able to identify that the visitors to Cardinal Place are almost exactly a third of each of office workers, local residents and tourists. To understand the needs, wants and desires of each target audience we engaged with multiple local stakeholder groups.

During RIBA Stage 2, a co-design process with local school children was facilitated by 2-3 Degrees. These young people helped inform the zoning of spaces, colour palette and planting that you see today at Cardinal Place. We also undertook pre-planning consultation that reached 3,821 total community members, including a public exhibition attended by over 350 people. To ensure our customers were heard, we also presented our initial ideas to office occupiers and retail occupiers around the estate and their feedback, including placement of trees to retain key views of retail signage, were incorporated.

Through 2024 and early 2025, the BD Landscape Architects' scheme was delivered. The works were also supplemented by an artist team led by Maich Swift Architects and Cardinal Place is now home to *The Invisible Compass* by Fabio Lattanzi Antinori and *Wind Vane* by Eva Berendes. These pieces, combined with the landscaping improvements, have revitalised the previously tired space into an area with real intrigue and a place where all stakeholders can come together.

Anecdotal feedback has been overwhelmingly positive, all areas being used by office workers during their breaks, school children and passers-by. Although it is still early to draw direct conclusions, monitoring equipment used across Cardinal Place has shown a +6% lunchtime footfall in January 2025 compared to January 2024 and sales for January-April 2025 were +5% from the previous year. This data suggests that we are achieving our aims of stimulating increased footfall and that footfall is also leading to longer dwell time and more spend. The provision of additional seating, a more calming atmosphere amongst planting and the intrigue of the newly commissioned public art could all be seen as contributing factors.

The feedback both qualitative and quantitative from Cardinal Place provides tangible evidence of the benefit derived from improvements to the urban realm. We will continue to monitor usage and collate evidence to help inform future public realm improvement schemes across the portfolio.

[1] European Office Occupier Sentiment Survey 2024

Richard Sansom is a Senior Project Manager in Landsec's Capital Projects team. Richard specialises in commercial major projects and delivery of Landsec's portfolio enhancement projects, including public realm improvement schemes.

Rich Sansom
(Senior Project Manager, Landsec)

8 The Practice

About Us

BD landscape architects are an award winning practice, committed to the integration of sustainable design in this *Climate Emergency* to deliver amazing & resilient places for people.

Our approach combines contemporary sustainable design with creative ecology looking to glean the unique genius loci from each place – our designs draw inspiration from the history, ecology, environment, use & character of the site.

We believe in creating **extraordinary effects** with *ordinary things* to deliver meaningful and much loved public spaces & places.

Reconnecting people with nature is one of our great challenges - working with imaginative clients and creative disciples of architecture, engineering and ecology we form intrinsic links between these collaborators to deliver innovative, biodiverse and beautiful places.

Giving everyone a voice is at the heart of what we do - we welcome input from local communities/ stakeholders and believe this is the best and most satisfying means to deliver a successful and original scheme in which everyone can take pride and have a sense of ownership.

We have strong experience working on a number of high profile squares, public realm regeneration, residential and education sector projects from inception though to delivery on site.

In 2022 we won 3 national Landscape Institute awards including 'outstanding overall winner' for our trailblazing work on Lovedon Fields – adding to our 15 national Landscape Institute awards over the past 7 years.

Timeline

2015

BD's inaugural study tour to Copenhagen. 2015 saw the official opening of the groundbreaking Pond Club at King's Cross. Two of our projects were published; Emmanuel Primary School in 'Great Schools' guidance by the AJ and LSBU in a book on 'Public Landscape'.

2016

Our first Landscape Institute award win for our BD journal vol i with Passport. 2016 featured team highlights of a London study tour, group swim in the Pond Club and completion of Lovedon Fields. Helen was promoted to Senior Landscape architect. BD and pH+ self build & fund 'The Milkshake Tree for 2016 London Festival of Architecture to raise awareness for the LCCCP charity.

2017

An amazing achievement picking up prizes at the LI awards for Pond Club and Lovedon Fields and brilliant study trip to Lyon. Emma promoted to Senior Landscape Architect having passed pathway to chartership and Chris joined the team.

2018

Our London studio launch and study tour of our completed projects at King's Cross. The entire office ran the Tewkesbury Half Marathon for charity and Helen was promoted to an Associate. Team site visit Winchester for Lovedon Fields and Bombay Saphire Distillery.

2022

Lizzie and Nikki join the team and company profiled in Landezine as only the third UK landscape practice to be included! BD pick up overall outstanding winner in the 2022 LI awards and study tour to Manchester. First BD social at Elephant Park and Lovedon Fields wins national RIBA awards and shortlisted for Neave Brown Award for Housing 2022. Sayer Street + the Meadow part of Open House London.

2021

Guto joins the team as an Associate and Rob appointed to the Design Council as an expert advisor. Lindsay passes RHS Horticulture Level 2 exams. Study tour to local Gloucestershire projects and studio profile in the compendium `Urban Landscape' alongside LSBU and Sayer Street. The Meadow formed part of 2021 London Festival of Architecture.

2020

The team goes remote during the global pandemic and Cat joins the team as Senior Landscape Architect. The Meadow opens at Elephant Park + post lockdown the team tour around the Living Wetland Theatre. Design work starts for Fidelity's campus, Sayer Street starts on site and BD form part of founding signatories to `Landscape Architects Declare'.

2019

Rob presented keynote lecture at Leeds Beckett University and hosted the Cheltenham Design Academy in the studio. Emma was promoted to an Associate and Jenna joined the team as Senior Landscape Architect. Lovedon Fields lead case study in new RIBA book on `Building in Arcadia'.

2023

Helen and Emma promoted to Senior Associates and team study tour to Oslo. Cardinal and WWT Slimbridge pick up highly commended LI awards and Glassfields a Designverse award. BD host a LISW student tour and codesign Cardinal Place with youth steering group.

2024

Jenna and Cat promoted to Associates and Nikki and Chris to Senior Landscape Architects. Brilliant tour and stay with the Newt in Somerset. BD projects published in 'The Meanwhile City' 'Public London' and 'Landscape Architecture Korea'.

2025

Rob speaks at UKreiiF in Leeds alongside current and future Landscape Institute presidents and presents a module for Architecture Today's School of Specification. BD winners at Regenerative Architecture Index Awards and shortlisted for SGLD awards. Study trip to London and epic Autumn social. Nefeli, Emma joins the team and Guto promoted to Senior Associate.

Press

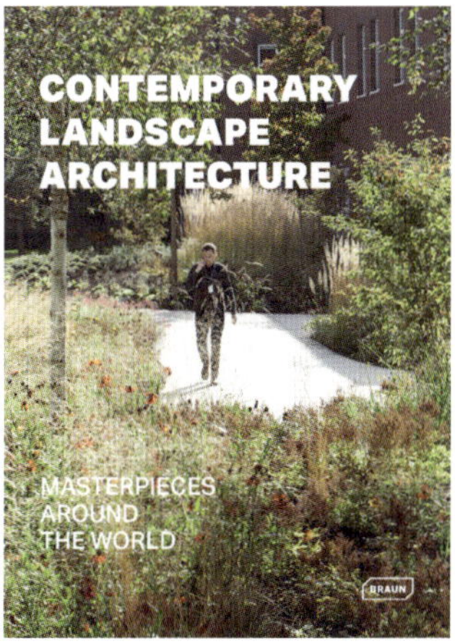

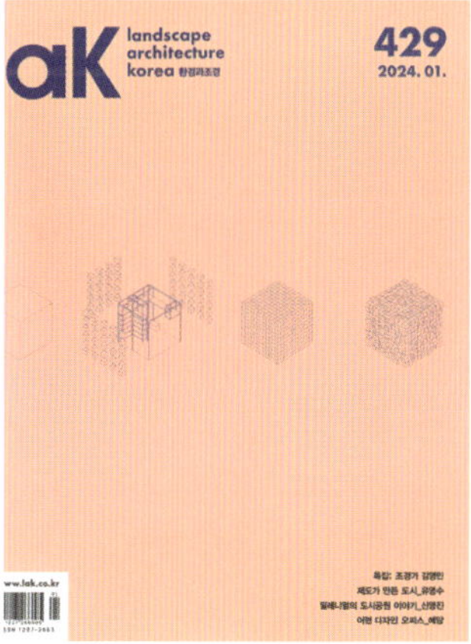

Beginning from top row, left to right:
1. Public Landscape Street Furniture ii (Hi-Design Publishing) 2. #Great Schools – Making the case for great design 3. BD landscape architects review journal i (self-published, 2015) 4. Buidling in Arcadia (Ruth Reed) 5. Urban Landscape (Cayetano Cardelús Vidal, 2001) 6. Meanwhile City (Milk & Petra Marko, 2022) 7. Architecture Today (Mar/Apr 2022) 8. Contemporary Landscape Architecture (Braun) 9. laK: Landscape Architecture Korea, Issue 429

The Difficult Teenage Years

by Rob Beswick (BD)

Reflecting back on the last 15 years in practice has been bitter sweet. Volume i of our review journal that spanned 2010-2015 was full of optimism for the future and hope of better things to come... little did we know about the difficult teenage years!

Landscape architects are, I think, eternal optimists so it has been difficult at times to stomach the past decade – the self-flagellation of Brexit, the covid pandemic, war in Europe and the increasing fraying of society and deterioration of natural systems and the climate.

Recessions, austerity and low productivity coupled with crippling price rises and inflation after Russia's invasion of Ukraine have moth-balled brilliant projects, folded great practices and bankrupted forward thinking developers.

The once-in-a-century global pandemic was perhaps the least foreseeable event and marked a real shift in the way we think and the ways we work. Lockdown made us stop and reflect, slow our pace of life, and [whilst searching the skies for vapour trails] opened our eyes to the beauty of nature, our ears to birdsong, and turned 3 million more Brits to their gardens.

Speaking with residents of Elephant & Castle, at our meanwhile Meadow, over a long weekend during the London Festival of Architecture in 2021 made me realize the true value of landscape. This pocket park formed the only accessible open space for many families during lockdown – this doorstep playable green lung with highlights of seasonal wildflower meadow and cherished public art brought fresh air, play, contact with nature and an uplifting sense of place to so many people during such a difficult time.

There is a joy to still seeing our work develop from those initial sketches, through planning and onto construction. Our co-design project at Cardinal Place, with 25 local young people over 6 months, felt like true codesign in action. There is a real joy in designing with communities and making tangible change.

I am prouder than ever of our exceptionally talented team of landscape architects led by Emma, Helen and Guto.

Furthermore I'm filled with great pride witnessing what we have achieved over the past decade – winning 3 national landscape institute awards in 2022 – and picking up the 'overall outstanding winner' prize were tremendous successes for a team as small as ours.

It will be a mark of the next decade to see how Artificial Intelligence impacts landscape architecture; whether it helps or hinders is yet to be realised. Additionally we are yet to know how the *design by numbers* approach for Biodiversity Net Gain can be integrated holistically into our projects, and how value engineering can be tempered to allow landscape to act as the glue that successfully binds together places.

I hope the examples in this journal serve as clear evidence for landscape as a catalyst for change.

Listening to Sir David Attenborough first hand in 2019 at the LI awards drilled the message home –

"Landscape architects have a great responsibility to bring the realities of the natural world, to the understanding and the love of human beings worldwide".

I'd like to take this opportunity to thank all of the amazing contributors to this journal, our brilliant team and the clients & collaborators who have kept us so busy for the past 15 years!

A huge thanks goes to the team that have helped forge the success of BD over the years.

Present Employees:
Cat Thomas
Chris Richardson
Emma Barnard
Emma Santamaria
Guto Jones
Helen Kirk
Jenna Watkins
Lindsay Beswick
Lizzie Rimmer
Nikki Petrova
Nefeli Papageorgiou
Mel Webb
Rob Beswick

Past Employees:
Aleksandra Jakuszewska
Catrin Menzies
Clem Whalley
Dimitrije Jankovic
Don Ward
Ella Scott
Holly Birtles
Jared Gibley
Jack Dilworth
Jacob Jenkins
Juliette Grondin
Sarah Carson
Stefanos Sampaziotis

Rob founded BD landscape architects in 2009 having worked in London, Chicago, Bristol & Bath as a project landscape architect on many prestigious and award winning schemes.

As the founder and director of BD, Rob's interest lies in innovative contemporary design that can be seen evolve from sketches on the drawing board through the public engagement, planning and construction processes to finished projects on site enjoyed by the public that leave a sustainable legacy for the future.

Rob Beswick
(Founder, BD)

ISBN 978-1-0369-3327-2

Front Cover Image: Living Wetland Theatre & Waterscapes Aviary

Special thanks to Cat Thomas for help drawing together and Jo Beswick + Helen Kirk for proof reading.

Incredible photography by Jack Hobhouse + Jim Stephenson and four illustrations by Marguerite Charles.

Book design and layout by
Design Office of Jonathan Finch
jfdesignoffice.com

Printed in the UK by Print Love
printlove.uk

All paper in this book is FSC® certified and produced using renewable energy. The white sheet used for the inner pages (Fedrigoni Arena HD) is made of pure ECF cellulose (bleached without chlorine). The cover material (Favini Crush) incorporates organic, leftover residues from fruit, nuts and grains to replace 15% of cellulose from trees alongside 40% post-consumer recycled fibre and cellulose from well managed forests.

BD landscape architects
Sun Street
Tewkesbury
GL20 5NX

bdlandarch.com
info@bdlandarch.com
@bd_landscape